C. Mulcahy

D0785145

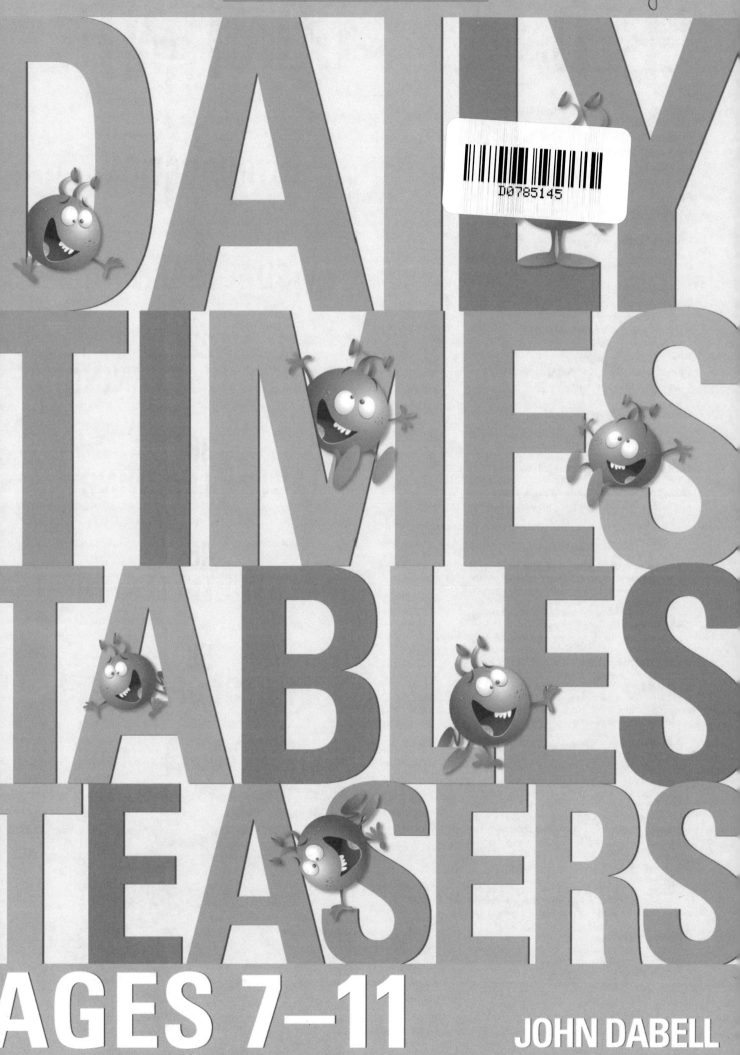

DAILY TIMES TABLES TEASERS

AGES 7–11

JOHN DABELL

CREDITS

Author
John Dabell

Illustrations
Nick Diggory

Development Editor
Kate Pedlar

Series Designer
Anna Oliwa

Editor
Kim Vernon

Designer
Mike Brain Graphic
Design Limited, Oxford

Project Editor
Fabia Lewis

Text © John Dabell
© 2007 Scholastic Ltd

Designed using Adobe InDesign

Published by Scholastic Ltd
Villiers House, Clarendon Avenue,
Leamington Spa, Warwickshire CV32 5PR

www.scholastic.co.uk

Printed by Bell and Bain Ltd

1 2 3 4 5 6 7 8 9   7 8 9 0 1 2 3 4 5 6

British Library Cataloguing-in-Publication Data
A catalogue record for this book is available from the
British Library.

ISBN 978-0439-94544-8

CONTENTS

INTRODUCTION

DAILY TIMES TABLES TEASERS FOR AGES 7-11

WHAT IS *DAILY TIMES TABLES TEASERS*?

Daily Times Tables Teasers 7–11 is a collection of activities designed to develop children's knowledge, skills and understanding in multiplication. The activities are linked to the requirements of the Primary Framework for mathematics for Key Stage 2.

The times tables teasers include games, rhymes, practical investigations and simple problem-solving tasks. The ideas are designed to be used flexibly and many can be easily adapted to reflect children's particular interests or to make cross-curricular links. In addition, most of the activities can be easily differentiated to cater for differing ability levels within a class.

HOW IS IT ORGANISED?

It is widely accepted that teachers need to use a range of presentation styles and teaching materials to ensure that all children are given the opportunity to learn through their preferred learning style.

The times table teasers are organised into four chapters, each focusing on a different learning style:

1. Visual (seeing)
2. Auditory (hearing)
3. Tactile (touching)
4. Kinaesthetic (moving)

WHAT DOES EACH TIMES TABLE TEASER CONTAIN?

To make the book easy to use, all the times table teasers follow the same format.

Learning objectives: Each times tables teaser addresses one or more of the NNS objectives.

Learning link: Many of the activities are multi-sensory. Links to other learning styles are listed in this section.

Organisation: Each times tables teaser gives suggestions for organisation, for example, whole class/small group. However, many of the ideas can be easily adapted for individual circumstances.

Resources: The resources needed to implement an activity are listed in this section.

What to do: Clear, step by step instructions are given for carrying out the activity. Emphasis is placed on active participation by the children through, for example, the use of games and practical apparatus. Where appropriate, suggested questions and opportunities for teacher interventions are also included.

Now try this: At the end of each times tables teaser, suggestions have been given for how to further develop or adapt the ideas in future lessons.

HOW TO USE THE ACTIVITIES

The times tables teasers are designed to provide ideas for short, purposeful activities that cater for the range of learning styles. They can be used in a number of ways.

1. Develop a daily times table teaser time, for example at the start of each day or after lunch.

2. Incorporate times table teasers into the daily maths lesson.

3. Choose an activity from each chapter in rotation or plan to focus on a different learning style each week to ensure that all learning styles are given equal coverage.

4. Many of the activities are teacher-led; others can be given to the children themselves for self-directed learning. It may also be appropriate for teaching assistants working within a class to conduct activities with smaller groups of children.

NEWS AT TEN

OBJECTIVE: to improve ability to multiply by 10
LEARNING LINK: auditory
ORGANISATION: whole class; groups of four
RESOURCES: the following, drawn on the board

WHAT TO DO

● Talk to a maths buddy about multiplying by 10. What happens to a number when it is multiplied by 10? Do you know any rules about multiplying by 10? Write them down.

● Share your ideas with the rest of the class.

● Look at the speech bubbles shown in the concept cartoon.

● Work in groups of no more than four and discuss the concept cartoon together. Which statements do you agree with and why?

● Share your ideas with the rest of the class. Did you agree or disagree with any of the statements in the cartoon? Have anyone's opinions changed since looking at the cartoon together?

● The rule for 'adding a zero' onto the end of a number when multiplying by 10 doesn't always work. Look at some examples of multiplying decimals together. Start with 1.0 × 10, 2.5 × 10, 10.0 × 10, and so on. Write your own examples in groups.

● Look at the concept cartoon conversation again. The decimal point is like a fixed concrete post – it never moves! The digits move, *not* the decimal point.

NOW TRY THIS

1. Invent some word problems that involve multiplying by 10, for example *If a CD holder contains 12 CDs, how many CDs do 10 CD holders contain? Each box contains 16 cans of cola. How many cans are there in 10 boxes?*

2. Think of situations when multiplying by 10 doesn't make a number ten times bigger, such as 0 × 10, 1 × 10.

THAT'S MAGIC

OBJECTIVE: to improve ability to multiply any number
LEARNING LINK: auditory
ORGANISATION: maths buddies
RESOURCES: calculator; pencils and paper

WHAT TO DO

● Write down the number 12345679 on a piece of paper.

● Now say a number between 1 and 9, for example 5.

● Multiply this number by 9 in your head:
5 × 9 = 45

● Write the product beneath the first number:
12345679
     × 45

● Use a calculator to work out the sum.

● The product (55555555) will be a row of the number chosen.

● The trick works with any digit. Try it several times with other numbers.

NOW TRY THIS

● On a calculator, key in 37037.

● Choose a number from 1 to 9, for example 4.

● Multiply whatever number you choose by 3:
3 × 4 = 12

● Now multiply 37037 × 12 = 444444.

CALCULATOR WORDS

OBJECTIVE: to improve ability to multiply any number
LEARNING LINK: auditory
ORGANISATION: maths buddies
RESOURCES: calculator; pencils and paper. Write the following numbers and letters on the board: 4, 3, 7, 7, 0 (h, E, L, L, 0).

WHAT TO DO
● Look at the numbers and letters on the board – the letters are actually calculator numbers turned upside down.
● Look at the following maths problems and their associated clues.
Use this to travel over snow 3691×125
Eat too quickly $1021 \times 371 + 15$
A synonym for a pig $50 \times 12 + 4$
A swan is part of the same family 17503×2
A famous theatre in London 3173×12
We like these at Easter $195 \times 29 + 8$
Wobbly $(130 \times 135) + (23 \times 3 \times 11 \times 23)$
Spill $5 \times 601 \times 5 \times 3$
● Turn your calculator upside down and read the words made.
● The first pair to find all the words are the winners.

Sleigh

Hog

Eggs

NOW TRY THIS
Make up your own calculator words, using multiplication.

I SPY

OBJECTIVE: to improve ability to multiply any number
LEARNING LINK: auditory, tactile
ORGANISATION: groups of four
RESOURCES: a collection of 0–9 number cards

WHAT TO DO
● Shuffle the cards well.
● Deal out the cards number face up in a 8×8 square (or any arrangement you choose).

4	8	5	1	9	8	7	3
4	2	5	6	7	9	1	4
2	5	3	8	6	7	4	4
5	2	7	9	1	3	5	2
3	5	6	8	9	5	7	4
7	2	4	3	1	5	9	8
2	5	1	4	7	2	8	3
8	3	5	9	7	8	5	1

● One member of the group is the 'I spy captain' with the other members acting as players.
● The captain calls out a multiplication product, for example, *I spy with my little eye 56*.
● Players have to spot two numbers that are adjacent to each other (vertically, horizontally or diagonally) that make the 'I spy number' by raising their hands quickly and pointing to the two cards. They take the cards.
● As cards are taken throughout the game, the captain needs to reposition the others so that they are next to each other.
● The player with the most cards at the end of the game is the winner.

NOW TRY THIS
1. Use cards showing larger numbers. The captain calls out the sum, *I spy with my little eye 7×7*. The players then look for the number that makes the answer.
2. Introduce fraction cards such as ½ and ¼ to make the game more challenging. Try adding negative number cards too.

TURN OVER

OBJECTIVE: to improve ability to multiply any number
LEARNING LINK: auditory, tactile
ORGANISATION: groups of four or pairs
RESOURCES: two sets of 0–9 number cards

WHAT TO DO

● Shuffle the number cards and place them face down in a pile.
● Take turns to turn over two cards.
● Multiply the numbers showing – this is your score.
● Keep a running total of your score.
● The first player to reach 250 or more is the winner (the target number can be anything you want).
● Award double points if you turn over any two numbers that are the same, for example 5 × 5 = 25 points – doubled makes 50 points.
● The opposition player(s) checks the winner's total using a calculator.
● Shuffle the cards and play again.

NOW TRY THIS

Play with three sets of cards.

SPLAT

OBJECTIVE: to improve ability to multiply by 2, 5 and 10
LEARNING LINK: auditory, tactile
ORGANISATION: groups of four or pairs
RESOURCES: one normal dice and one labelled ×2, ×2, ×5, ×5, ×10, ×10; coloured counters; a gameboard (see below)

WHAT TO DO

● Each player has a collection of coloured counters – for this game they are called 'splats'.
● Roll the two dice and find the product.
● Now look for the product on the gameboard. If it is there then you can splat it with a counter.
● The winner is the first player to get four splats in a line vertically, horizontally or diagonally.

12	25	2	40	21	12	40
8	30	2	6	20	30	50
6	15	8	25	30	20	6
30	60	9	5	4	6	60
25	50	25	30	10	20	5
8	4	5	6	25	30	4
20	50	30	2	15	6	60

NOW TRY THIS

Instead of covering four numbers in a line, change the rules so that the winner has to get three in a line anywhere on the board.

FOUR IN A ROW (1)

OBJECTIVE: to improve ability to multiply any number
LEARNING LINK: auditory, tactile
ORGANISATION: groups of four or pairs
RESOURCES: two dice, one marked 3, 4, 5, 6, 7, 8 and the other marked 4, 5, 6, 7, 8, 9; coloured counters; a gameboard (see below)

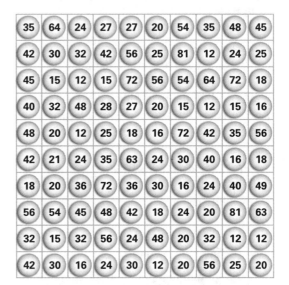

35	64	24	27	27	20	54	35	48	45
42	30	32	42	56	25	81	12	24	25
45	15	12	15	72	56	54	64	72	18
40	32	48	28	27	20	15	12	15	16
48	20	12	25	18	16	72	42	35	56
42	21	24	35	63	24	30	40	16	18
18	20	36	72	36	30	16	24	40	49
56	54	45	48	42	18	24	20	81	63
32	15	32	56	24	48	20	32	12	12
42	30	16	24	30	12	20	56	25	20

WHAT TO DO

● Roll both dice and find the product.
● Cover the product with a counter.
● If your product isn't on the board or has already been covered, wait until your next go.
● The first player to get four in a row either vertically, horizontally or diagonally is the winner.

NOW TRY THIS

Use a 0–100 square and play with three dice, one marked 3, 4, 5, 6, 7, 8 and two marked 4, 5, 6, 7, 8, 9. Roll two dice and multiply together. Then roll the third dice and subtract this number from the product.

NUMBERBALL

OBJECTIVE: to improve ability to multiply any number
LEARNING LINK: auditory, tactile
ORGANISATION: groups of four or pairs
RESOURCES: five dice; coloured counters; a playing board (see below)

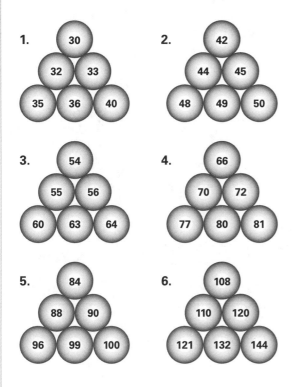

1.
30
32 33
35 36 40

2.
42
44 45
48 49 50

3.
54
55 56
60 63 64

4.
66
70 72
77 80 81

5.
84
88 90
96 99 100

6.
108
110 120
121 132 144

WHAT TO DO

● Throw one dice – the number thrown indicates which 'Numberball' pyramid you will play.
● Now throw the other four dice in two groups of two.
● Add up the numbers in each of the two groups and multiply the two totals together.
● If possible, place a counter on the football that shows your product.
● If you make a numberball that appears at the top of the pyramid, have another go.
● The first player to have at least one counter in each of the six groups of balls is the winner.

NOW TRY THIS

Try adding another row to each pyramid or add another 'Numberball pyramid' made up of numbers of your own choosing.

FACTOR FIND

OBJECTIVE: to improve ability with factors
LEARNING LINK: auditory
ORGANISATION: groups of four or pairs
RESOURCES: a dice, 0–9 number cards; copies of grids (see below)

WHAT TO DO

● Roll the dice twice and write the numbers thrown inside any of the four boxes.

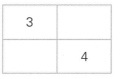

3	
	4

● Now turn over two number cards and write these numbers inside the other two boxes.
● When the boxes have been filled, this makes four two-digit numbers (two rows and two columns).
● Now work out how many factors each number has. For example:

3	6
0	4

The factors of 36 are: 1, 2, 3, 4, 6, 9, 12, 18, 36
The factors of 04 are: 1, 2, 4
The factors of 30 are: 1, 2, 3, 5, 6, 10, 15, 30
The factors of 64 are: 1, 2, 4, 8, 16, 32, 64
● Add the total number of factors together to make the overall score. In the example above, the score is 27.
● The winner is the player with the largest score after five games (you could make the winner the person with the lowest score or alter the number of games you play).

NOW TRY THIS

Change the scoring so that if you make a square number you score an extra 4 points.

BOXING

OBJECTIVE: to improve ability to multiply any number
LEARNING LINK: auditory
ORGANISATION: groups of four or pairs
RESOURCES: 0–9 number cards; copies of grids (see below)

WHAT TO DO

● Turn over a number card and write the number inside one of the boxes. Do this three more times.

3	×	4
7	×	6

● Now multiply the numbers made – there are three that go across and three that go down.

3	×	4	=	12
×		×		×
7	×	6	=	42
=		=		=
21	×	24	=	504

● The total score is the product in the bottom right-hand box.
● Play this five times and add up the total score for each game.
● The winner is the player with the largest total.

NOW TRY THIS

Investigate whether swapping around the four numbers inside the boxes makes a difference.

MUDDLES

OBJECTIVE: to improve ability to multiply any number
LEARNING LINK: auditory
ORGANISATION: maths buddies
RESOURCES: none required

WHAT TO DO

● Write out ten multiplication problems and their products.
● Muddle each one up and write the numbers on a separate piece of paper, for example 4 × 8 = 32 could be 3428.
● When you have muddled your multiplications, swap papers with a buddy and try to work out what each multiplication equation could be.

NOW TRY THIS

Work out the multiplication muddles for numbers larger than 10, for example 12 × 4 = 48 could be written as 41248.

LETTERSWORTH

OBJECTIVE: to improve ability to multiply any number
LEARNING LINK: auditory
ORGANISATION: maths buddies
RESOURCES: none required

WHAT TO DO

● Write down the numbers 0–9. Underneath them, write down letters of the alphabet in any order, for example:

```
0  1  2  3  4  5  6  7  8  9
F  B  G  M  E  T  Y  O  V  D
```

● Now write out one of the times tables using this code, for example:
1 × 7 = 7 would be B × O = O
2 × 7 = 14 would be G × O = BE
● Ask your maths buddy some times tables questions using the code. For example, *What is V × M? It's GE*, and so on.

NOW TRY THIS

Give each letter of the alphabet a number, for example A = -1, B = -2, and so on, and multiply different letters together.

ODDBALL

OBJECTIVE: to improve ability to multiply any number
LEARNING LINK: auditory
ORGANISATION: maths buddies
RESOURCES: none required

WHAT TO DO

- Look at these numbers:

5306

8253

7426

4369

6488

- Spot which is the odd one out. Why?
- Each number is a number sandwich. Look carefully at the beginning and end numbers and relate those to the numbers in between. Can you spot a multiplication? (for example $5 \times 6 = 30$)
- Create your own versions for your friends to spot and present them to the class.

NOW TRY THIS

Invent oddball teasers that focus on the times table you need the most practice in. For example, the six-times table 6244, 9546, 6498, 3186, 6366.

ANSWERS
Various answers may be suggested to the first part of this activity. They should all be valued.

PRODUCT PLACEMENTS

OBJECTIVE: to improve ability to multiply any number
LEARNING LINK: auditory
ORGANISATION: maths buddies
RESOURCES: 0–9 number cards; 6 × 10 grids

WHAT TO DO

- Players share the same 6 x 10 grid.
- Shuffle the 0–9 number cards and place them face down in a pile.
- Player 1 takes a card from the pile and places it face up anywhere on the grid.
- Player 2 does the same.
- The idea of the game is to make rows of sums that make multiplication equations so decisions have to be made about where to place the numbers.
- Players keep on taking turns trying to make correct equations.
- Once a card has been placed it cannot be moved.

- Every correct multiplication made scores points equal to the product.
- Compare your score with another pair. The pair with the most points wins.

	X		=	5	
	X		=		
	X	7	=	2	
3	X		=		
	X		=		
	X		=		
	X		=		
9	X		=	1	1
	X		=		
	X		=		

NOW TRY THIS

Modify the rules so that players are allowed to discard three cards during the course of a game. You could also change the scoring system so that the digital root of the score equals the points.

WHAT A HAND!

OBJECTIVE: to improve ability to multiply any number
LEARNING LINK: auditory
ORGANISATION: maths buddies
RESOURCES: five sets of 0–9 number cards

WHAT TO DO

- Shuffle five sets of 0–9 number cards.
- Deal out eight cards to each player.
- Place the remaining cards face down in a pile – this forms the stock.
- The aim of the game is to make sets of multiplication equations, such as 3721 ($3 \times 7 = 21$) and 9654 ($9 \times 6 = 54$), and so on.
- Draw a single card and place it face up next to the stock – this is the discard pile.
- Each player draws a card from the stock or discard pile.
- They decide to keep or discard the picked-up card. If they keep it, they must discard one of their other cards.
- Whenever a player has four cards that make a multiplication equation, these are placed on the table and four new cards are picked up from the stock.
- The game continues until the stock pile runs out.
- The winner is the player with the most equations.

NOW TRY THIS

Change the game so that the first player to make three sets of equations is the winner.

COMMON MULTIPLES

OBJECTIVE: to recognise the multiples of 3 and 4
LEARNING LINK: auditory
ORGANISATION: maths buddies
RESOURCES: photocopiable page 58: Multiplication grid; coloured pencils

WHAT TO DO

● Colour all the multiples of 3 on your multiplication grid in the same colour.
● Now colour all the multiples of 4 in another colour.
● Why are some numbers coloured in both colours?
● These are common multiples.
● Find all the common multiples of 3 and 4 up to 100.

NOW TRY THIS

Colour in the multiples of other numbers such as 5 and 2 – what common multiples can you find?

1	2	3	4	5	6	7	8	9	10
2	4	6	8	10	12	14	16	18	20
3	6	9	12	15	18	21	24	27	30
4	8	12	16	20	24	28	32	36	40
5	10	15	20	25	30	35	40	45	50
6	12	18	24	30	36	42	48	54	60
7	14	21	28	35	42	49	56	63	70
8	16	24	32	40	48	56	64	72	80
9	18	27	36	45	54	63	72	81	90
10	20	30	40	50	60	70	80	90	100

OUT OF SIGHT

OBJECTIVE: to improve ability to multiply any number
LEARNING LINK: auditory
ORGANISATION: maths buddies
RESOURCES: photocopiable page 58: Multiplication grid; pieces of shaped card

WHAT TO DO

● A multiplication grid is projected onto the board.
● Discuss how it is made up. Can you spot any patterns and describe them?
● Your teacher covers some of the numbers with a piece of shaped card, for example a T-shape (the T-shape needs to cover five numbers going across and six down)
● Which numbers are covered? How did you work them out?

● Now work with your maths buddies and do the same, using different shapes to cover the numbers.

NOW TRY THIS

Rotate the times table squares through 90°, 180° and 270°.

1	2	3	4	5	6	7	8	9	10
2	4	6	8	10					
3	6	9	12	15	18	21		27	30
4	8	12	16	20	24	28		36	40
5	10	15	20	25	30	35		45	50
6	12	18	24	30	36	42		54	60
7	14	21	28	35	42	49		63	70
8	16	24	32	40	48	56	64	72	80
9	18	27	36	45	54	63	72	81	90
10	20	30	40	50	60	70	80	90	100

COMMON DOTS

OBJECTIVE: to improve ability to multiply by 2, 3 and 5
LEARNING LINK: tactile, auditory
ORGANISATION: maths buddies
RESOURCES: copies of circles marked with numbers 0–24 around the circumference and 24 and 0 sharing the same point (see below); rulers; coloured pencils

WHAT TO DO

● Start at zero and count around the numbers in the five-times table. Join each number to the next number in the table using a ruler and a red pencil.
● Now do the same for the three-times table using a blue pencil.
● Use a green pencil for the two-times table.
● What patterns can you see?
● Write down the numbers that are joined by more than one coloured line.
● Multiples that are common to two or more numbers are said to be common multiples. For example:
Multiples of 2 are 2, 4, 6, 8, 10, 12, 14, 16, 18…
Multiples of 3 are 3, 6, 9, 12, 15, 18…
● So, common multiples of 2 and 3 are 6, 12, 18 and so on.

NOW TRY THIS

Point out the common multiples of 2 and 5.

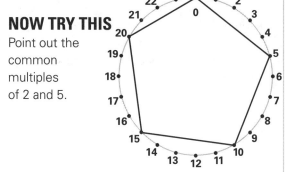

GOTCHA!

OBJECTIVE: to improve ability to multiply any number
LEARNING LINK: auditory
ORGANISATION: maths buddies
RESOURCES: target boards (see below)

WHAT TO DO
● The following target board is on the board.

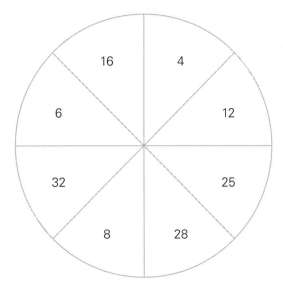

● The class divides into two teams.
● See if your team can spot the following:
A number with 6 factors
A square number
The square root of 36
A multiple of 8
The product of 8 and 4
Five sets of 5
A factor of 18
The first common multiple of 4 and 6
The quotient of 24 divided by 3
● The team to answer correctly scores that number of points.

NOW TRY THIS
Invent your own target circles and questions for another group to try.

ANSWERS
A number with 6 factors = 28, 32
A square number = 4, 16, 25
The square root of 36 = 6
A multiple of 8 = 16, 32
The product of 8 and 4 = 32
Five sets of 5 = 25
A factor of 18 = 6
The first common multiple of 4 and 6 = 12
The quotient of 24 divided by 3 = 8

GRID WORK

OBJECTIVE: to improve ability to multiply any number
LEARNING LINK: tactile, auditory
ORGANISATION: groups of four
RESOURCES: product grids; photocopiable page 60: Factor sheet; dice; counters; paper and pencils

WHAT TO DO
● Divide a group of four into two teams, the red team and blue team.
● Each team has a product grid like this to share and some red or blue coloured counters.

six y	7	20	36	35	18	100
five y	21	16	25	54	45	4
four y	14	8	42	12	72	20
three y	50	27	49	54	15	3
two y	10	6	28	63	36	32
one y	18	13	48	50	81	5
	one x	two x	three x	four x	five x	six x

● Toss a coin to see who starts, for example, the red team.
● The red team throws one dice – this is the x number. They then throw the next dice – this is the y number.
● They then read their x, y coordinate number (remember, along the corridor and up the stairs). For example, if they threw a 3 and then a 4, their x, y number would be 42. They cover this number with a red counter.
● If a team lands on a square already covered by a counter, they miss their go.
● The red team then tries to find all the factors of 42. If they can find them all, they score 42 points.
● The blue team check the factors by looking on the factor sheet.
● The blue team now have their go and hand the factor sheet to the red team for checking their answer.
● The game ends after each team have had six throws each.
● The winning team is the team with the most points.

NOW TRY THIS
Award extra points for teams who make four in a row either vertically, diagonally or horizontally.

VISUAL LEARNING

SPIDERGRAMS

OBJECTIVE: to improve ability to multiply any number
LEARNING LINK: auditory
ORGANISATION: whole class or groups
RESOURCES: photocopiable page 60: Factor sheet

WHAT TO DO

● There is a diagram on the board like this:

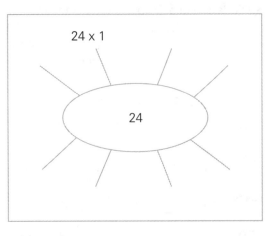

24 x 1

24

● Suggest multiplication facts to complete the spidergram.
● Write each one at the end of the spider's legs.
● Write your multiplications in two different ways, for example 6 × 4 and 4 × 6.

NOW TRY THIS

Draw another spidergram on the board with a different number in the centre. Find all the factors that make up that number. Write the numbers at the end of the spider's legs. Have a go on your own and find the factors for your age, house number, today's date and so on. All numbers have an even number of factors except square numbers. All square numbers have an odd number of factors.

CARROLL DIAGRAMS

OBJECTIVE: to improve ability to multiply any number
LEARNING LINK: kinaesthetic
ORGANISATION: pairs
RESOURCES: Carroll diagram charts (see below)

WHAT TO DO

● The following Carroll diagram is drawn on the board:

	Prime	Not prime
Even	1 x 7 30 ÷ 2	8 x 6
Not even	3 x 3 20 ÷ 5	3 x 0

● In pairs, look at the multiplication and division sums inside each part of the Carroll diagram. Are they all in the right place? Should any be moved?
● Write three more sums inside each box for another group to look at. Can they work out if they are accurate or not?
● Create your own versions using different categories, for example:

	Even	Not even
Divisible by 4	12 14	6 9
Not divisible by 4	1 10	5 25

NOW TRY THIS

Turn your Carroll diagrams into displays outside the classroom for others to look at. Can they spot which numbers are out of place?

NUMBER NAMES

OBJECTIVE: to improve ability to multiply any number
LEARNING LINK: kinaesthetic
ORGANISATION: whole class or groups
RESOURCES: paper and pencils

WHAT TO DO

- The name 'Eliza Periwinkle' is written on the board. Copy it onto a piece of paper.
- Now count the number of vowels and the number of consonants and then multiply the two together.
- So, Eliza Periwinkle has 7 vowels and 8 consonants which is $8 \times 7 = 56$
- Work out the values of other names. For example, Amelia Bedelia, Canyon String, Conroy Billaboo, Periwinkle Hop, Jagdish Jingle, Everest Pink, Judson Fudge, Kariza Karunahoo, Mungo Milton, Polly Pooper, Roland Skylark, Felix Funk, Ziggy Blastpop, Cosmo Twoshoes.
- Select celebrity names and work out their products.
- Work out how many factors each product has.

NOW TRY THIS

Can you find someone in the class with the same product value as your own name?

ON THE DOUBLE

OBJECTIVE: to improve ability to multiply any number
LEARNING LINK: auditory
ORGANISATION: whole class or groups
RESOURCES: paper and pencils

WHAT TO DO

- Ancient Egyptians sometimes multiplied using a kind of base-2 arithmetic. For example, to multiply 7×13 make two columns.
- Start with 1 and 7 (one of the numbers we want to multiply). Then we double the number in each column, over and over until we get to a number just below the other number (13 in this case) in the left-hand column.

1	7
2	14
4	28
8	56

- The powers of two are in the left column, and 7 times the powers of two are in the right column.

- You make 13 out of the numbers in the left column, by adding $8 + 4 + 1$. That is where the base-2 arithmetic comes in.
- Place a pencil mark next to 8, 4 and 1 and add up the numbers in the second column $7 + 28 + 56 = 91$
- Practise other one-digit x two-digit examples together to get familiar with the method.

NOW TRY THIS

When you have practised the doubling method, you can try calculating harder examples, for example 20×12, 34×19, 31×25, 90×64, and so on.

FOUR IN A ROW (2)

OBJECTIVE: to improve ability to multiply any number
LEARNING LINK: auditory, tactile
ORGANISATION: maths buddies
RESOURCES: number grid (see below); three dice; different-coloured counters

WHAT TO DO

- Each player takes a turn to roll three dice and multiply together the numbers thrown. For example, 2, 4 and 6 would make $2 \times 4 \times 6 = 48$
- If the answer is on the board, the player covers it with a coloured counter.
- The winner is the first player to get four counters in a row.

8	4	16	64	48	36	75	12
60	12	60	120	24	8	125	72
12	72	10	216	4	30	27	24
36	90	40	100	24	20	2	40
15	12	36	1	90	6	64	24
6	60	20	75	48	5	150	40

NOW TRY THIS

Change the rules. The first player to place six counters wins or the first player to place the most counters in four minutes wins. This game can be made less competitive by getting players to work together to cover three rows or 12 counters.

DIVIDED WORDS

OBJECTIVE: to use vocabulary associated with division
LEARNING LINK: auditory
ORGANISATION: maths buddies
RESOURCES: number sentences (see below)

WHAT TO DO

● Fill in the spaces with the correct words from the word box.

The _____ is the number you are dividing by.
The answer to a division sum is called the _____ .
Dividing a number by four will give you a _____ of that number.
An amount left over when one number is divided by another number is called the _____ .
The _____ is the number being divided.
Division is the _____ of multiplication.
Dividing a number by ten will give you a _____ of that number.
Division can be regarded as repeated _____ .
Division can be thought of as 'sharing' or _____ .

WORD BOX
quarter, grouping, quotient, reverse, subtraction, remainder, dividend, divisor, tenth

NOW TRY THIS

Create your own number sentences for multiplication words.

ANSWERS
divisor, quotient, quarter, remainder, dividend, reverse, tenth, subtraction, grouping

CRACK THE CODE

OBJECTIVE: to improve ability to multiply any number
LEARNING LINK: auditory
ORGANISATION: maths buddies
RESOURCES: code and multiplication sums (see below)

WHAT TO DO

● Look at the multiplication sums with your maths buddy and then follow the code.
● Solve each sum and translate this into a letter. What does the sentence spell?

8 × 0
4 × 4
3 × 7
15 × 2
6 × 5
3 × 6
8 × 6
9 × 7
2 × 9
7 × 4
6 × 3
30 × 1

A	B	C	D	E	F	G
21	6	54	12	63	90	5

H	I	J	K	L	M	N
16	18	81	9	35	48	42

O	P	Q	R	S	T	U
64	4	11	72	28	30	56

V	W	X	Y	Z
45	0	10	27	77

ANSWER
0 = W
16 = H
21 = A
30 = T
30 = T
18 = I
48 = M
63 = E
18 = I
28 = S
18 = I
30 = T
What time is it?

NOW TRY THIS

Create your own codes for specific multiplication or division sums, or a mixture of both.

FACTOR TREE

OBJECTIVE: to improve ability to multiply any number
LEARNING LINK: auditory
ORGANISATION: maths buddies
RESOURCES: paper and pencils

WHAT TO DO

- Grow a factor tree together.
- Begin by planting a product, for example 36.

36

- Next decide on two factors for your product – these are the first row of branches in your factor tree.

9   4

36

- Now find factors for the first row of numbers.

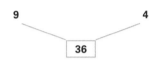

3   x   3   x   2   x   2

9   4

36

- Keep finding factors until the only factors left are one.
- All the factors in the last row of the tree should equal 36.
- Now look at these factor trees and fill in the missing numbers.

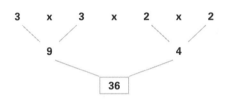

6

24

5

60

4

32

NOW TRY THIS

Try growing your own factor trees for other numbers, for example 48, 54, 64, 72.

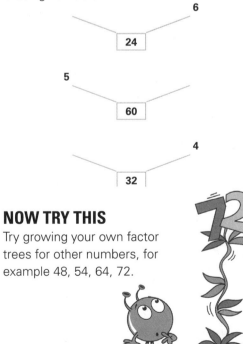

MULTIPLICATION GRIDS

OBJECTIVE: to improve ability to multiply any number
LEARNING LINK: auditory
ORGANISATION: maths buddies
RESOURCES: photocopiable page 58: Multiplication grid; pencils; rulers; squared paper

WHAT TO DO

- Use a multiplication grid to help you work out the missing numbers on the multiplication grid fragments below.

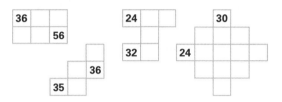

- Draw your own table fragments using squared paper.

NOW TRY THIS

Look at the multiplication grid and try to spot patterns together.

ALPHA-ZULU

OBJECTIVE: to improve ability to divide by any number
LEARNING LINK: auditory
ORGANISATION: maths buddies
RESOURCES: none required

WHAT TO DO

- Write out the letters of the alphabet and number each one, a = 1, b = 2, c = 3, and so on.
- Now work out the answers to the following division problems and translate into words:
32/2 36/2 90/10 76/4 52/4
300/100 100/4 24/2 81/9 28/2 40/10 75/15 90/5
45/3 200/100 144/12 120/8 154/11 49/7

NOW TRY THIS

Invent your own division problems. Target specific spellings or specific vocabulary, for example science words.

ANSWERS
16, 18, 9, 19, 13 = prism
3, 25, 12, 9, 14, 4, 5, 18 = cylinder
15, 2, 12, 15, 14, 7 = oblong

SORT IT OUT

OBJECTIVE: to improve ability to multiply/divide any number

LEARNING LINK: auditory

ORGANISATION: maths buddies

RESOURCES: Venn diagrams (see below)

WHAT TO DO

● Look at the Venn diagram with your maths buddy.

● Another group has started to fill the Venn in but they are not sure about their answers – is what they have filled in correct?

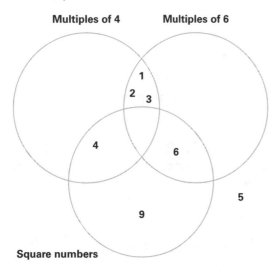

● Can you complete the Venn for all the numbers from 1–30?

NOW TRY THIS

Invent your own triple-ring Venn diagrams for other multiples.

PATIENCE

OBJECTIVE: to improve ability to multiply any number

LEARNING LINK: auditory

ORGANISATION: maths buddies

RESOURCES: playing cards

WHAT TO DO

● Remove the picture cards from the deck of playing cards.

● Deal four cards face up and place the rest face down.

● Now turn over one card at a time from the deck and place it under any of the four other cards.

● Remove the column when it adds up to a multiple of 10.

● The winner is the player with the most cards at the end of the game.

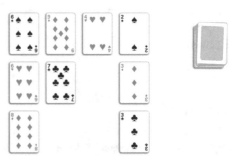

NOW TRY THIS

Instead of a multiple of 10, focus on a different multiple, such as 12.

MULTIPLES

OBJECTIVE: to improve ability to multiply any number

LEARNING LINK: auditory

ORGANISATION: maths buddies

RESOURCES: multiple boards for each pair (see below); counters; dice

WHAT TO DO

12	18	15	6	12	6
24	9	12	9	18	30
18	6	12	9	18	30
24	12	6	30	3	24
18	12	6	3	24	18
6	18	3	12	30	3

● Take turns to roll a dice – one player multiples their score by 3 and covers the answer on the board.

● The other player multiplies their score by 6 and covers the answer on the board.

● The winner is the player who can get four counters in a line.

NOW TRY THIS

After the best of three, players swap over and multiply by a different number. Can you invent your own multiple board using a different set of numbers?

CHINESE MULTIPLICATION

OBJECTIVE: to improve ability to multiply any number
LEARNING LINK: auditory
ORGANISATION: maths buddies
RESOURCES: Chinese multiplication grids

WHAT TO DO

- This is an alternative way of multiplying called Chinese multiplication or 'Gelosia' lattice multiplication.
- Draw a grid like this

- Complete the grid by multiplying top and side numbers.

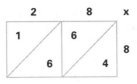

- Now add the diagonal numbers starting from the right.

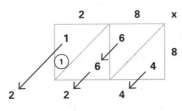

- Remember to add the tens into the next diagonal.

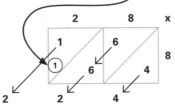

- Practise multiplying a number of double-digit and single-digit numbers in this way.

NOW TRY THIS

Progress to multiplying three-digit by two-digit numbers.

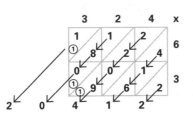

TRIPODS

OBJECTIVE: to improve ability to multiply any number
LEARNING LINK: auditory
ORGANISATION: maths buddies
RESOURCES: paper and pencils

WHAT TO DO

- Look at the number tripods onto the board and think what the missing numbers could be.

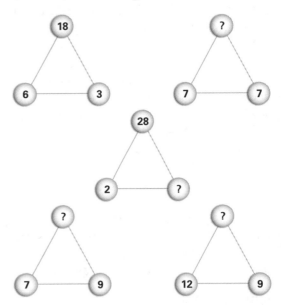

Write out the division and multiplication facts for each one. For example:

$18 \div 3 = 6$
$18 \div 6 = 3$
$3 \times 6 = 18$
$6 \times 3 = 18$

NOW TRY THIS

Invent more challenging tripods for your friends to try.

ANSWERS
$7 \times 7 = 49$
$49 \div 7 = 7$

$2 \times 14 = 28$
$28 \div 14 = 2$
$14 \times 2 = 28$
$28 \div 2 = 14$

$7 \times 9 = 63$
$63 \div 9 = 7$
$63 \div 7 = 9$
$9 \times 7 = 63$

$12 \times 9 = 108$
$108 \div 12 = 9$
$108 \div 9 = 12$
$9 \times 12 = 108$

HAPPY NUMBERS

OBJECTIVE: to improve ability to multiply any number
LEARNING LINK: auditory
ORGANISATION: maths buddies
RESOURCES: pencil and paper; photocopiable page 59: Hundred square

WHAT TO DO

- Take any number, such as 23.
- Square each of the digits and add them together: 2 squared + 3 squared = 4 + 9 = 13
- Now split 13 and square these digits: 1 squared + 3 squared = 10
- Now split 10 and square: 1 squared + 0 squared = 1
- 23 is a happy number because it ends in 1.

$23 - 2^2 + 3^2 = 4 + 9 = 13$
$13 - 1^2 + 3^2 = 1 + 0 = 10$
$10 - 1^2 + 0^2 = 1 + 0 = 1$

- Investigate other numbers to see whether they are happy or not.
- Split into working groups and find all the happy numbers from 1–100 and circle them on a 1–100 grid. For example, one group takes the numbers from 1–10, the next group 11–20, and so on.

NOW TRY THIS

Investigate numbers beyond 100. Are there an infinite number of happy numbers? Are there an infinite number of unhappy numbers?

> **ANSWERS**
> There are 20 numbers from 1–100 that are happy numbers, they are: 1, 7, 10, 13, 19, 23, 28, 31, 32, 44, 49, 68, 70, 79, 82, 86, 91, 94, 97, 100

DIGITAL ROOTS

OBJECTIVE: to improve ability to multiply any number
LEARNING LINK: auditory
ORGANISATION: maths buddies
RESOURCES: 11 × 11 number square, filled out as opposite; pencils and paper

WHAT TO DO

- Digital roots are calculated by adding the individual digits of a number. For example, the digital root of 132 is 6 because 1 + 3 + 2 = 6. The digital root of 29 is 2 because 2 + 9 = 11 and 1 + 1 = 2.
- Find the digital roots of all the times tables up to 10 × 10 by filling out the following table.
- Look for patterns – what do you notice?

x	1	2	3	4	5	6	7	8	9	10
1	1	2	3	4	5	6	7	8	9	1
2	2	4	6	8	1	3	5	7		
3										
4										
5										
6										
7										
8										
9										
10										

NOW TRY THIS

Investigate the digital root patterns for times tables up to 15.

MIND READER

OBJECTIVE: to improve ability to multiply any number
LEARNING LINK: auditory
ORGANISATION: maths buddies
RESOURCES: photocopiable page 59: Hundred square

WHAT TO DO

- Ask your maths buddy to choose a section of the hundred square that is five rows wide and five rows deep. For example:

1	2	3	4	5	6	7	8	9	10
11	12	13	14	15	16	17	18	19	20
21	22	23	24	25	26	27	28	29	30
31	32	33	34	35	36	37	38	39	40
41	42	43	44	45	46	47	48	49	50
51	52	53	54	55	56	57	58	59	60
61	62	63	64	65	66	67	68	69	70
71	72	73	74	75	76	77	78	79	80
81	82	83	84	85	86	87	88	89	90
91	92	93	94	95	96	97	98	99	100

- Tell your buddy that you can add all the numbers inside the square faster than anyone else in the class.
- You can use a calculator or use a pencil and paper method.
- The trick here is to look at the middle number in the square and then multiply it by 25:
$38 \times 25 = 950$
- Tell your buddy how you did this so quickly. Discuss why you think it works
- Try the trick again.

> **ANSWER**
> This method works because 38 is the mean number of a range of numbers that go up at regular intervals.

FIVES

OBJECTIVE: to improve ability to multiply any number
LEARNING LINK: auditory
ORGANISATION: maths buddies
RESOURCES: pack of playing cards; number grid (see below); coloured counters

WHAT TO DO

● Take out all the Jacks, Queens, Kings and Aces from the playing cards.
● Shuffle the cards and place them face down.
● Take turns to turn over a card, multiply the number by 5 and cross out the product on the grid below.

35	20	45	10	50	40	5	30
50	45	30	25	35	25	20	5
25	15	5	10	10	40	15	30
45	25	40	35	5	15	40	50
15	5	35	25	10	50	30	15

● The winner is the first player to cross out four in a row in any direction.

NOW TRY THIS

To practise another times table, alter the grid to show the appropriate multiples.

YOUR CALL

OBJECTIVE: to improve ability to multiply any number
LEARNING LINK: auditory
ORGANISATION: maths buddies
RESOURCES: a number grid (see below)

WHAT TO DO

Multiple of 4	Odd number	Square number	Between 50 and 60
Prime number	Digital root 2	Multiple of 6	Even number
Less than 7	First digit 5	Last digit 9	Three-digit number
Number divisible by 3	Number divisible by 10	Multiple of 8	Between 10 and 30

● Fill in your own 4 by 4 grid with numbers that match the above.

● Double check your buddy's grid by discussing the numbers in each box.
● Now go round the class. Each child says a number of their own choice.
● If that number is on your grid, then cross it off.
● The winner is the first player to cross off all their numbers.

NOW TRY THIS

Make the number grid smaller or larger and change the types of numbers.

DIVISION SPIDER

OBJECTIVE: to improve ability to divide any number
LEARNING LINK: auditory, tactile
ORGANISATION: maths buddies
RESOURCES: a spider picture (see below); 0–9 number cards; paper and pencils

WHAT TO DO

● Look at the spider picture.

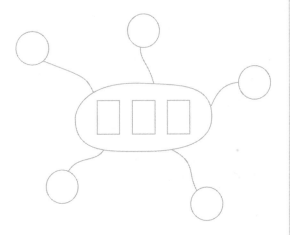

● Shuffle the cards, then deal three of them. Place them face up inside the spider.
● Rearrange the digits inside the spider to make numbers that are exactly divisible by the numbers on the legs.
● Points are awarded as follows: 12 points for each correct answer, 25 bonus points for numbers divisible by 7, 4 bonus points for numbers divisible by 2, 5 or 10.

NOW TRY THIS

Instead of five legs, increase or decrease accordingly. Have a four-digit number in the centre of the spider's body and alter the points system.

TABLE COORDINATES

OBJECTIVE: to improve ability to multiply any number
LEARNING LINK: auditory, tactile
ORGANISATION: maths buddies
RESOURCES: squared paper or graph paper

WHAT TO DO

- Write out a particular times table as a set of coordinates. For example, for the six-times table these would be: 6 (0,6) 12 (1,2) 18 (1,8) 24 (2,4) 30 (3,0), and so on.
- Plot these points onto square paper as follows:

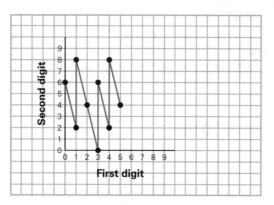

- Compare the graphs and the pattern that the six-times table has made.
- Investigate the patterns made by other times tables.

INSIDE OUT

OBJECTIVE: to improve ability to multiply any number
LEARNING LINK: auditory, tactile
ORGANISATION: maths buddies
RESOURCES: examples of hexagons below

WHAT TO DO

- Look at the hexagon of numbers.
- Find the perimeter and interior.

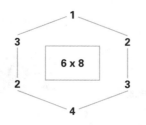

- To find the perimeter, multiply all the numbers that make up the outside circumference: $1 \times 2 \times 3 \times 4 \times 2 \times 3 = 144$.
- To find the interior, multiply the two numbers in the middle together: $6 \times 8 = 48$.

- Once you have found the perimeter and interior, try to find a connection between the two numbers (the outside number is three times bigger than the inside number).

NOW TRY THIS

Follow the same method and try the following examples.

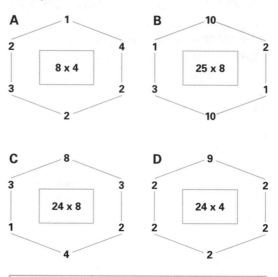

ANSWERS
A Perimeter = 32   Interior = 32
B Perimeter = 600   Interior = 200
C Perimeter = 574   Interior = 192
D Perimeter = 288   Interior = 96

TABLE SEARCH

OBJECTIVE: to improve ability to multiply any number
LEARNING LINK: auditory, tactile
ORGANISATION: maths buddies
RESOURCES: table grid (see below)

WHAT TO DO

- Look at the table grid.
- Circle any times table sums you can see:

1	x	8	=	5	7	=	3	x	3	8
3	x	6	4	x	4	x	x	x	x	=
x	=	6	x	=	x	3	6	6	x	6
6	x	5	=	3	6	=	=	=	3	x
=	5	x	6	5	=	x	1	5	4	3
2	x	6	=	1	2	x	8	=	5	2
4	5	=	6	x	4	=	3	6	=	x
4	6	3	=	6	x	6	=	2	6	6
x	3	0	6	=	6	x	0	1	x	=
3	x	6	=	6	5	=	6	x	9	9

- Invent your own version of the grid for the seven-, eight- and nine-times table.

NOUGHTS AND CROSSES

OBJECTIVE: to improve ability to multiply any number
LEARNING LINK: auditory, tactile
ORGANISATION: maths buddies
RESOURCES: photocopiable page 60: Factor sheet; a dice labelled 3, 4, 5, 6, 7, 8

WHAT TO DO

● Play this with your maths buddy.
● One player draws a noughts and crosses grid.
● The dice is rolled – lowest number starts.
● Roll the dice. If you roll a 5, you can place any number from the five-times table inside the grid.
● The number you choose is important. Choose a number according to the numbers of factors it has got. So if you write down 15, this number has four factors. Use your factor sheet to help you.
● Player two rolls the dice. For example, 3. This player writes down any number from the three-times table anywhere on the grid. For example, 21. This number has 4 factors as well.
● Continue taking turns. The idea of the game is to get a row of numbers either vertically, horizontally or diagonally with the same number of factors. For example, the following grid shows a winning line because all the numbers have four factors.

15		
	21	
		27

NOW TRY THIS

Restrict the game to getting a row of numbers with a specific number of factors, for example four factors only.

DOUBLE TROUBLE

OBJECTIVE: to improve ability to multiply any number
LEARNING LINK: auditory, tactile
ORGANISATION: maths buddies
RESOURCES: number boxes (see opposite)

WHAT TO DO

● Look at the number boxes on the board.
● Multiply the numbers in the top box by 6. Place the products in the left-hand box.

● Multiply the numbers in the top box by 7. Place the products in the right-hand box.
● Double the numbers in both boxes.
● Subtract the smaller number in the doubles boxes from the larger number.
● Finally, add all the numbers together and then write out all the factors of this number.

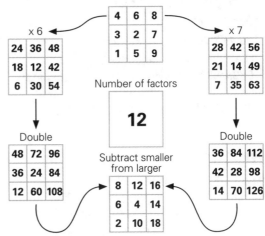

NOW TRY THIS

Investigate other numbers.

TIMES DESIGN

OBJECTIVE: to improve ability to multiply any number
LEARNING LINK: auditory, tactile
ORGANISATION: maths buddies
RESOURCES: circles (see below)

WHAT TO DO

● Look at the following times-table pattern.
3 6 9 12 15 18 21 24 27 30 33 36
● Remove the 'units' from each number. For example:
3 6 9 2 5 8 1 4 7 0 3 6
● Now using the circle below, join these numbers together. What do you notice?

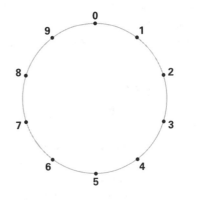

NOW TRY THIS

● Investigate the pattern made for the four-, five-, six- and seven-times tables.

CLEVER ELEVEN

OBJECTIVE: to improve ability to multiply by 11
LEARNING LINK: visual, tactile
ORGANISATION: whole class; small groups; maths buddies
RESOURCES: pencils and paper; calculators

WHAT TO DO

● Improving ability to multiply any two-digit number by 11 in your head is easier than it looks. To work out 17 × 11, add the 1 and 7 to make 8 and then place this number in between 17 to make 187.

● Talk through some more examples in small groups and practise multiplying numbers by 11 up to 18.

● What happens when multiplying 11 by 19? Does this method still work? If, not, can you think of a way you could do it?

● If the sum of the units digits is 10 or greater, the one is carried. For example, 11 × 19 would be 1 + 9 = 10. Placing 10 in between 1 and 9 would make 1109 which would be too high. Instead, carry the 1 and add it to the other 1 to make 2. So the answer is 209.

● Try a number of harder examples, such as 11 × 38, 11 × 56, and so on, to practise carrying the 1.

● With your maths buddy, teach each other what to do. One partner describes the process and the other partner closes their eyes and tries to mentally visualise each step, that is, adding, separating and carrying.

● Have a brain vs calculator competition by setting up some × 11 calculations. One of you use your brain and the other a calculator. Who is fastest at calculating the sums?

NOW TRY THIS

Multiplying 11 by bigger numbers is more demanding but follows the same adding method. For example, to calculate 11 × 543, you add 5 and 4 to make 9 and then add 4 and 3 to make 7. The 9 and 7 are then inserted in between 5 and 3 to make 5973. Check on your calculators to make sure this is right!

MULTIPLE PILE UP

OBJECTIVE: to improve ability to multiply and divide any number
LEARNING LINK: visual
ORGANISATION: maths buddies
RESOURCES: none required

WHAT TO DO

● Write out the numbers from 1–9 in any order, for example, 938217654.

● Separate the digits with commas, for example 938,217,654.

● Read out the number: nine hundred and thirty-eight million, two hundred and seventeen thousand, six hundred and fifty-four.

● Now work out a number of things about your number, such as:

  ● Is your number a multiple of 5? How do you know?

  ● Is your number divisible by 4? How do you know?

  ● Is your number divisible by 3? How do you know?

Look through tests of divisibility together, for example:

Divisibility tests	Example
A number is divisible by 3 if the sum of the digits is divisible by 3.	237 is divisible by 3 because the sum of the digits is 12 (2 + 3 + 7 = 12), and 12 is divisible by 3.
A number is divisible by 4 if the number formed by the last two digits is divisible by 4.	316 is divisible by 4 because 16 is divisible by 4.
A number is divisible by 6 if it is divisible by 2 and it is divisible by 3.	168 is divisible by 6 because it is divisible by 2 and it is divisible by 3.
A number is divisible by 8 if the number formed by the last three digits is divisible by 8.	7,120 is divisible by 8 because 120 is divisible by 8.
A number is divisible by 9 if the sum of the digits is divisible by 9.	549 is divisible by 9 because the sum of the digits is 18 (5 + 4 + 9 = 18), and 18 is divisible by 9.

NOW TRY THIS

Investigate other tests of divisibility.

LISTEN IN

OBJECTIVE: to improve ability to multiply any number
LEARNING LINK: visual, kinaesthetic
ORGANISATION: whole class; small groups
RESOURCES: pencils and paper

WHAT TO DO

● Learn some of the following rhymes to help remember times tables:

Six asked eight for a date, 6 × 8 makes 48
My flight! My flight! I'm gonna be late!
'We're boarding now from gate 6 × 8!'
6 × 8? That's 48!
Gate 6 x 8, that's 48,
that's my gate! I'm going to be late!
Store in my brain box 48

I found two sevens stuck on a sign
Multiplied them together and made 49
7 × 7 makes 49,
that's why they stuck them on the sign
Store in my brain box 49

I found eight 8s sitting on the floor
I picked 'em up
Now I've got 64!
8 × 8, that's 64
back on the floor, say no more, 64, 64, 64!
Store in my brain box 64

4 said to 7
Do you think I'm overweight?
7 said to 4
You look like 28
28? 28? He's so overweight!
4 × 7 makes 28
Store in my brain box 28

● Invent your own verses to share with the rest of the class. Using bingo names can be useful, for example:

Cup of tea 3 (3 × 1)
Tom's tricks 6 (6 × 1)
Buckle my shoe 32 (8 × 4)
Clean the floor 54 (6 × 9)
Winnie-the-Pooh 42 (7 × 6)

NOW TRY THIS

Hold a class competition to see who can come up with the most inventive rhymes.

PLIP PLOP

OBJECTIVE: to improve ability to multiply any number
LEARNING LINK: kinaesthetic
ORGANISATION: whole class; small groups
RESOURCES: none required

WHAT TO DO

● Play this active listening game in small groups or as a whole class. It is sometimes called 'Times tables snap' or 'Fizz buzz'.
● Count forward in unison, at a steady rate. When you reach 3 or a multiple of 3, say *plip* instead of the number word:
One, two, plip, four, five, plip, seven, eight, plip and so on.
● Repeat the activity for multiples of 6, except this time when you reach 6 or a multiple of 6, say *plop*. So the sequence will be:
One, two, three, four, five, plop, seven, eight, nine, ten, eleven, plop.
● Now bring both activities together so that multiples of both 3 and 6 become *plip plop* too:
One, two, plip, four, five, plip plop, seven, eight, plip, ten, eleven, plip plop and so on.
● If anyone makes a mistake, the game continues.
● Vary the multiples and invent your own number names or play the game in French, German, or any other language. You could also add actions, or clap in rhythm.
● There is no need to start at 1 and you can vary activities to include primes, squares, and so on.

NOW TRY THIS

A suitably challenging and enjoyable version of this game is 'plip plop poopa scoopa' which extends the plip plop game. Any prime number is replaced by *poopa* and any multiple of 7 is replaced by *scoopa*, for example:
One, poopa, plippoopa, four, poopa, plip plop poopa scoopa, eight, plip, ten, poopa, plip plop, and so on.

EGGSACTLY

OBJECTIVE: to improve ability to multiply by 6
LEARNING LINK: visual, tactile
ORGANISATION: small groups
RESOURCES: a 1–10 dice or 1–10 spinner

WHAT TO DO

● Roll a 1–10 dice. Read out the number and say, *I've thrown five egg boxes.*
● Discuss how many eggs there would be in five egg boxes.
● Repeat the process a number of times.
● Record answers in a table, for example:

Egg boxes	Eggs
5	30
6	36
2	12

NOW TRY THIS

1. Ask and answer questions such as, *I wonder how many eggs there are in 7 boxes?* and *If there are 48 eggs, how do I work out how many egg boxes that is?*
2. To practise multiples of 4, choose cars and wheels; for multiples of 5, choose hands and fingers.

TAPE IT

OBJECTIVE: to improve ability to multiply any number
LEARNING LINK: visual
ORGANISATION: maths buddies
RESOURCES: tape recorder; cassette tapes; headphones; answer sheet for each child

WHAT TO DO

● Recorded on tape are ten multiplication problems using silly words, for example 7 wibbles × 4 wobbles = 28 wibble wobbles, 3 clips × 8 clops = 24 clip clops, 5 toots × 9 boots = 45 toot boots
● Record your answers on the sheet your teacher will give you.
● Listen to the tape – complete your answers with your maths buddy.

● Create your own times table test for recording.
● Play to the whole class and test them.

NOW TRY THIS

Replace the silly words for more meaningful real-world examples. Record your work on the computer.

TRIO

OBJECTIVE: to improve ability to multiply/divide any number
LEARNING LINK: visual
ORGANISATION: small groups
RESOURCES: pencils and paper

WHAT TO DO

● Work in small groups. Your teacher will read out a list of statements about the number trio 3, 5 and 15 for you to remember. You can't write anything down.

Fifteen is three lots of five.
Five times three gives fifteen.
If I multiply three and five I get fifteen.
Three into fifteen goes five.
Fifteen divided by three equals five.
Three and five are factors of fifteen.
Fifteen is a multiple of three and it's also a multiple of five.
Fifteen is in the three- and five-times tables.
Fifteen is where the three-times table and the five-times table crash into each other.

● Listen to the list again. When it is finished, you have to write down everything you can remember about the trio 3, 5 and 15.
● Team up with another group to see if they have any statements written down that you don't have.

NOW TRY THIS

When you have worked on one number trio, focus on listening to another trio using similar statements. You can also add your own statements to the list for another group to remember.

MILLIONAIRE MATHS

OBJECTIVE: to improve ability to multiply/divide any number
LEARNING LINK: visual
ORGANISATION: maths buddies
RESOURCES: pencils and paper

WHAT TO DO

● Stage a maths version of the 'Millionaire' game. Here is the start of it.
● Read out the 'Fastest finger first' question followed by the questions for each amount of prize money:

Starting with the smallest, put these sums in order of size:
$6 \times 4, 28 \div 7, 5 \times 5, 4 \times 0$
Question 1: £100
What is 3×4? 21, 12, 13, 7
Question 2: £200
What is 6×0? 6, 60, 0.6, 0
Question 3: £500
What is $18 \div 2$? 36, 9, 14, 4
Question 4: £1,000
What is $30 \div 6$? 15, 5, 6, 4

● See if you can finish the game, writing up to the 15th question.
When you have written all the questions, play the game with another group.

NOW TRY THIS

Increase or decrease the number of options for each question.

WHO AM I?

OBJECTIVE: to improve ability to multiply/divide any number
LEARNING LINK: visual
ORGANISATION: small groups
RESOURCES: pencils and paper

WHAT TO DO

● Tell your group that you are a special number and it is their job to work out who you are.
● Provide them with clues and ask them to discuss what number they think you are.
● For example:

I am less than 25×3 but more than a baker's dozen.
I am a multiple of 7.
I am an odd number.
I am a square number.
Who am I?

I am more than 3×7 but less than 29.
I can be divided by 4 with a remainder of one.
Who am I?

I am an even number.
I am $< 8 \times 7$ but $> 4.5 \times 2$.
I have eight factors.
My units digit is double my tens digit.
Who am I?

NOW TRY THIS

Invent your own 'Who am I?' problems for your friends to solve.

ON THE TABLE

OBJECTIVE: to improve ability to multiply any number
LEARNING LINK: visual
ORGANISATION: maths buddies
RESOURCES: number box (see below); dice; different-coloured counters

WHAT TO DO

● Point to a number in the number box. Say an appropriate multiplication or division fact using this number. For example, if the number is 45, you might say, *5 lots of 9 are 45*.
● Practise this a few times until you know what to do. Then play against your maths buddy.
● One player rolls both dice. The first number rolled is the x number and the second number rolled is the y number. So, if a 1 and a 5 are rolled, then the number in that square is 0. The player has to say a fact associated with this number, for example $10 \times 0 = 0$. They cover the 0 with a counter in their colour.
● The first player to cover four boxes in a row is the winner.

6	3	7	72	63	4	144
5	0	45	36	72	81	24
4	27	54	50	36	6	9
3	100	21	8	70	7	25
2	10	18	42	30	56	121
1	70	16	54	45	12	90
	1	2	3	4	5	6

NOW TRY THIS

Instead of four in a row, this game could be played as the first player to cover a whole row or column is the winner, or the first player to cover four numbers in the five-times table, and so on.

CROP CIRCLES

OBJECTIVE: to improve ability to multiply any number
LEARNING LINK: visual
ORGANISATION: maths buddies
RESOURCES: crop circle patterns; photocopiable page 60: Factor sheet

WHAT TO DO

● Each pair has a factor list.
● Look at the circle pattern on the board. With your buddy, work out why the numbers have been placed in the way they have.

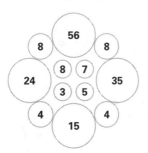

● This is how the numbers are arranged. The numbers in the small circles are multiplied together and the product is placed above or to the side in the large circles. Then, going clockwise, the medium circles next to the large ones show the number of factors for these products.
● Now solve the following crop-circle pattern.

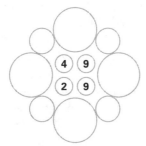

NOW TRY THIS

Design your own crop circles for your friends to try.

SWAPS

OBJECTIVE: to improve ability to multiply any number
LEARNING LINK: visual, tactile
ORGANISATION: maths buddies
RESOURCES: number cards 0–9; calculator

WHAT TO DO

● Shuffle your number cards.
● Deal out four cards to make a two-digit by two-digit calculation. Then work this out using a pencil and paper method or a calculator.

● Now rearrange the same digits to make a different multiplication sum.
● Find as many different products as you can by continuing to move the digits around. Talk about your ideas and verbalise your thinking as you work.
● When you have found all the different combinations, write out the smallest and largest products you can make with these digits.

NOW TRY THIS

You could change this activity to include a three-digit by two-digit multiplication sum.

REMAINS OF THE DAY

OBJECTIVE: to improve ability to divide any number
LEARNING LINK: visual, tactile
ORGANISATION: maths buddies
RESOURCES: dice; counters; *Snakes and ladders* gameboard

WHAT TO DO

● Maths buddies take it in turns to roll a dice.
● Whatever number is thrown, move that number of spaces.
● Now divide the number you land on by the number on the dice. Say the sum out loud.
● If the number you land on divides exactly, you don't score any points. If your number when divided has a remainder, the number of points scored is the number of the remainder.
● If you roll a five, have another go.
● If you get a remainder of three points, double this to make six.
● The winner is the player with the most points at the end of the game.

NOW TRY THIS

Invent your own gameboard and include three-digit numbers of your own choosing.

BINGO-BONGO

OBJECTIVE: to improve ability to multiply any number
LEARNING LINK: visual, tactile
ORGANISATION: whole class
RESOURCES: *Bingo-bongo* cards (see examples below); a set of multiplication flash cards (optional)

3		24	30		50		72
	12	25			54		
8		27		45		64	81
	16		36	49			

	16		32				
6		20		42	54	70	
	18	25		48		88	
9		28	35		60		121

			32				
4	15	21		42	60		
	16	24	36			64	81
6		27		48	66		100

		20		42		72	
6		27	32		60		100
8	18		36		64	77	
		28		48			121

	10		30				81
6		21		42	56	64	
		24	32	45			100
9	18	28				72	

WHAT TO DO

● Each player has a *Bingo-bongo* card.
● Your teacher will call out multiplication questions (or use multiplication flash cards) for you to cross off on your bongo cards.
● The first player to cross out the numbers in one row calls out *Bongo!* and scores 5 points.
● The first player to cross off all their numbers calls out *Bingo-bongo!* and scores 15 points.
● Play the game again.

NOW TRY THIS

This time you have a blank 6 x 6 grid to fill in. The game will be based on the four-, five- and six-times tables. You have to work out which numbers you should not write on your cards. Numbers such as 2, 3, 7, 9, 11, 13, and so on are not solutions to any maths facts that comprise the four-, five- or six-times tables.

BINGO-FLAMINGO

OBJECTIVE: to improve ability to multiply any number
LEARNING LINK: visual
ORGANISATION: small groups
RESOURCES: *Bingo-flamingo* cards (see examples below); dice; counters

1	12		34	45	
2		22			
	15	24	38	47	50

	14	26		40	
4		27	32		54
5	16		33		55

3		28	36	40	
	18	27		42	59
6	19	29			

WHAT TO DO

● Each player has a *Bingo-flamingo* card.
● Take turns to throw the dice.
● Look on your grid to see if there are any numbers that will divide exactly by this number.
● The first player to cover all their numbers wins the game by shouting *Bingo-flamingo!*

NOW TRY THIS

Increase the sizes of the numbers you write inside each cell of the bingo boxes.

DIVIDE AND CONQUER

OBJECTIVE: to improve ability to divide any number
LEARNING LINK: visual
ORGANISATION: maths buddies
RESOURCES: dice (labelled 4, 5, 6, 7, 8 and 9); an ordinary 1–6 dice; counters

WHAT TO DO

● Take it in turns to roll the (specially labelled) dice and multiply the two together.
● Your maths buddy then rolls one ordinary dice to find the divisor.
● Divide the product made by the divisor.
● If the number has a remainder, then this is your score. For example, if you rolled a 6 and 7, they multiply together to make 42. If the ordinary dice rolled was 5, then 5 goes into 42 eight times with a remainder of 2, so 2 points would be scored.
● The winner is the first player to reach 30 points.

NOW TRY THIS

Try playing with three ordinary dice.

MATHS RULES OK

OBJECTIVE: to improve ability to multiply any number
LEARNING LINK: visual
ORGANISATION: maths buddies
RESOURCES: dice (labelled 4, 5, 6, 7, 8 and 9); an ordinary 1–6 dice; counters

WHAT TO DO

● Look at the connected rows of numbers on the board (see below).
● Discuss what the missing number might be. Take time to discuss your ideas. The missing number can be worked out by finding a special rule.
● Go through an example as a class:

4	6	10	12	13	20
13	19	31	37	40	?

The rule is triple the number and add 1. The missing number here is 61.
Now find the rules for the following multiplication sums.

8	1	3	7	5
18	4	8	16	?

8	4	3	7	1
84	44	34	74	?

2	9	3	6	4	12
9	44	14	29	19	?

NOW TRY THIS

Once you have got the hang of this, make some rules up of your own that involve the four operations.

ANSWERS

8 1 3 7 5
18 4 8 16 12
The rule is: double the number and add 2.

8 4 3 7 1
84 44 34 74 14
The rule is: multiply the number by 10 and add 4.

2 9 3 6 4 12
9 44 14 29 19 59
The rule is: multiply the number by 5 and subtract 1.

QUADRALIX

OBJECTIVE: to improve ability to multiply any number
LEARNING LINK: visual
ORGANISATION: maths buddies
RESOURCES: none required

WHAT TO DO

● A monster has been discovered on the island of Pentacrux called a Quadralix, a hideous monster with four arms and four legs. Each arm has six claws and each foot has seven toes. A Quadralix also has five eyes.
● Talk to your maths buddy and work out:
  ● How many arms do two Quadralix have?
  ● How many eyes do four monsters have?
  ● How many toes do two monsters have?
  ● How many claws does one Quadralix have?

NOW TRY THIS

Invent your own maths monster with different features. Create your own questions as a challenge for the rest of the class.

RHYME AND REASON

OBJECTIVE: to improve ability to multiply any number
LEARNING LINK: visual
ORGANISATION: maths buddies
RESOURCES: pencils and paper

WHAT TO DO

● Read the following rhyme about multiplying by three:

Three plump robins
Chatting in a tree
One times three
Is only three!

Up poke some worms
Showing off their tricks
'Two threes', they say
'Are always six'

Tummies start to rumble
Bellies ready to dine
Three times three
Is most definitely nine!

● Continue this rhyme or invent one of your own for another times table.

NOW TRY THIS

Hold a rhyme and reason times table competition and display all rhymes on the wall for others to enjoy.

NUMBER RHYME

OBJECTIVE: to improve ability to multiply any number
LEARNING LINK: visual
ORGANISATION: maths buddies
RESOURCES: pencils and paper

WHAT TO DO

● Write out a particular times table all the way up to 10 × and say it out loud a number of times.
● Now write out a list of words that rhyme with the numbers at the end of each line.
● For example:

   5 Clive
   10 pen
   15 Mr Sheen
   20 plenty
   25 bee hive
   30 dirty
   35 duck and dive
   40 naughty
   45 twist and jive
   50 nifty

● Invent a story using these words.

NOW TRY THIS

Write out all your tables using rhyming words.

DIGITAL TALK

OBJECTIVE: to improve ability to multiply any number
LEARNING LINK: visual
ORGANISATION: maths buddies
RESOURCES: pencils and paper

WHAT TO DO

● Some say that 24 is a special number because it is four times the sum of its digits. For example, 2 + 4 = 6 and 6 × 4 is 24. Can you think of any other numbers under 50 that are four times the sum of their digits? Can you see a pattern?

● Now work out similar 'Who am I?' type questions. For example:

   I am the only number under half a century that is five times the sum of its digits.

NOW TRY THIS

Invent your own digit sums.

ANSWERS
The special numbers are: 12, 24, 36, 48
Answer to riddle: 45

PRODUCT DIFFERENCE

OBJECTIVE: to improve ability to multiply any number
LEARNING LINK: visual
ORGANISATION: maths buddies
RESOURCES: pencils and paper; number grid (see below)

WHAT TO DO

● Draw a 5 × 5 grid with numbers up to 25.
● Highlight any four numbers in the grid that make a square, for example

   14 15
   19 20

1	2	3	4	5
6	7	8	9	10
11	12	13	14	15
16	17	18	19	20
21	22	23	24	25

● Now multiply the numbers in opposite corners of the square.
● What is the difference between the two products?
● Try again with a different four numbers in the square.
● What do you notice about the difference between the products?
● Does this happen for other sizes of square?

NOW TRY THIS

Investigate a grid with six numbers in each row.

IN MY PLACE

OBJECTIVE: to improve ability to multiply any number
LEARNING LINK: visual
ORGANISATION: small groups
RESOURCES: a dice; 0–9 number cards

WHAT TO DO

● Draw three boxes like this:

● The aim of the game is to make the largest product possible by placing three digits inside three boxes – where to place them is a real game of strategy.
● Roll the dice for the first number. Place it where you think is best.
● Turn over a card for the second number.
● Finally, roll the dice again for the last number.
● Multiply the two-digit number by the one-digit number.
● Each group member has a go.
● Whoever has the largest product scores three points.
● Play a number of times. Add up the total scores to find the winner.

NOW TRY THIS

Increase the number of boxes so that it is three digits multiplied by one digit, or two digits multiplied by two digits. Anyone who makes a palindromic product scores a bonus five points.

EGG BOX MATHS

OBJECTIVE: to improve ability to multiply by any number
LEARNING LINK: visual, auditory
ORGANISATION: whole class
RESOURCES: egg boxes of different sizes (one for each child); counters, cubes or similar

WHAT TO DO

● Look at the problem written on the board, for example 3 × 5. Show this using different sections of your egg box. For example, you could use three compartments and put five counters in each of those compartments, or use five compartments filling each with three counters.
● Count your cubes in groups of 3 or 5 and extend the sequence verbally.
● The multiplication sign stands for groups of eggs.
● Try different examples remembering to show the groupings in two different ways.

NOW TRY THIS

Use larger egg trays such as the 12 ×12 cartons and practise bigger numbers. Alternatively, join smaller cartons together. Now find a range of multiplication sums and test each other.

A HANDY WAY TO MULTIPLY!

OBJECTIVE: to multiply by 9
LEARNING LINK: auditory, kinaesthetic
ORGANISATION: whole class and pairs sitting in two concentric circles
RESOURCES: two hands drawn on the board with the fingers labelled 1, 2, 3, 4, 5, 6, 7, 8, 9, 0 (see below); stickers to write the numbers on and then stick to their fingers (not all children will need this)

WHAT TO DO

● It is possible to multiply by 9 just using your fingers.
● Hold out your hands or place them face down on the table so that your thumbs point toward one another.
● Visualise that your left little finger stands for 1, the next finger 2, and so on left to right, until your right little finger stands for 0. Look at the drawing on the board.

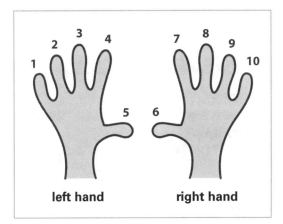

left hand   **right hand**

● Now use your fingers to multiply by 9. Try 4 × 9. Put the finger down that represents 4. All fingers to the left of the down finger represent the tens digit of the answer. You have 3 fingers up, so that makes 30. All the fingers to the right represent the ones digit. You have 6 fingers up, so the answer is 36.

Example: 4 x 9

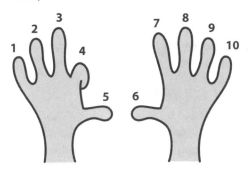

● Try this for other numbers by playing 'Show me'.

● Sit on chairs in two concentric circles whereby the inner circle faces outwards and the outer circle faces inwards. Everyone is facing a partner.
● Children in the outer circle call out a × 9 instruction for their partner in the inner circle to show with their hands, for example, *Show me 5 x 9*.
● Children in the inner circle then call out an instruction for their outer circle partner.
● After one minute, the outer circle stands and moves one place anti-clockwise to face a new partner. Take turns asking each other × 9 questions, as before.

NOW TRY THIS

1. Play 'Quick draw nines'. A × 9 fact will be called out. You have to do this as quickly as you can.
2. A small group of children could demonstrate 'A handy way to multiply' in assembly.

FOUR IN A ROW

OBJECTIVE: to improve ability to multiply up to 6 × 6
LEARNING LINK: visual, auditory
ORGANISATION: maths buddies
RESOURCES: a dice; 20 red and 20 blue counters or cubes; 1 × 6 number grid (see below)

WHAT TO DO

● This is a game for two players (or double up and play in a group of four as two teams).
● Work with a partner. Each player selects a coloured cube.
● Take turns to roll the dice.
● Cover a multiple of the number thrown. For example if you throw a 5 you can cover 5, 10, 15, 20, 25, 30, or 35. You can only cover one number at a time.
● The first player to cover four numbers in a line vertically, horizontally of diagonally is the winner.

1	2	3	4	5	6
7	8	9	10	11	12
13	14	15	16	17	18
19	20	21	22	23	24
25	26	27	28	29	30
31	32	33	34	35	36

NOW TRY THIS

1. Now play the game with two dice. Multiply the numbers thrown to cover one of the numbers on the board.
2. Design your own board with no redundant numbers.

TACTILE LEARNING

TIMES SQUARE

OBJECTIVE: to improve ability to multiply up to 6 × 6
LEARNING LINK: visual, auditory, kinaesthetic
ORGANISATION: maths buddies
RESOURCES: two dice; 20 red or blue counters or cubes; number grids (see below)

WHAT TO DO
- Throw the dice and multiply the numbers together.
- Use a cube to cover up the product on the board.
- If a double is thrown, this wins a bonus throw.
- The winner is the first player to cover a 2 × 2 square.

8	15	4	24	12	36
6	1	30	3	20	24
12	4	18	6	10	2
36	18	5	25	12	24
16	15	5	8	4	15
25	16	3	30	2	25

NOW TRY THIS
Vary the game to make the winning set: four in a line, a coloured cube on every row, a 3 × 3 'L' shape or an idea of your own making.

PELMATHISM

OBJECTIVE: to improve ability to multiply any number
LEARNING LINK: auditory
ORGANISATION: maths buddies
RESOURCES: multiplication and product cards for the seven- and eight-times tables (see below) cut out and shuffled, pencils and paper for keeping score

M		P	
7 x 1	8 x 1	7	8
7 x 2	8 x 2	14	16
7 x 3	8 x 3	21	24
7 x 4	8 x 4	28	32
7 x 5	8 x 5	35	40
7 x 6	8 x 6	42	48
7 x 7	8 x 7	49	56
7 x 8	8 x 8	56	64
7 x 9	8 x 9	63	72

WHAT TO DO
- Shuffle the multiplication and product cards.
- Place them face down and lay them out in front of you.

- Each player, in turn, turns over two cards – if the cards match, the player takes them and has another go. If they don't match then the cards are turned over and the other player has a go.
- The trick is to remember what's on each card and where each card is placed so that when you watch your partner, you can cunningly take note and clean up!
- Make sure that when you match cards, you say out loud what the multiplication equation is.
- Each player starts with 100 points – for every match you score 50 points. If you don't match then you lose 5 points.
- The winner is the player with the most points after all the cards have been matched.

NOW TRY THIS
Vary the game by having a set of cards with numbers on them and a set of cards showing symbols. You could focus on just one of the times tables or play snap as a simpler version. You could invent your own versions to take home to practise, or change the number of cards.

ALL HANDS ON DECK

OBJECTIVE: to improve ability to multiply any number
LEARNING LINK: auditory, visual
ORGANISATION: maths buddies
RESOURCES: a pack of playing cards; photocopiable page 58: Multiplication grid

WHAT TO DO
- Shuffle the cards and place them in a pile on the table.
- Player 1 turns two cards over for player 2 to multiply.
- Player 2 multiplies the two numbers together – the product made equals the number of points scored. Picture cards count as 10.
- Player 1 checks, using a multiplication square.
- Players take it in turns, keeping a running total of their scores.
- The game ends when all the cards have been turned over. The winner is the player with the most points.

NOW TRY THIS
The rules can be changed. Try, for example, any multiple of six scores an extra 20 points, two cards of the same suit score a bonus 10 points, two cards with the same numbers means miss a go, and so on.

TARGET PRACTICE

OBJECTIVE: to improve ability to multiply any number
LEARNING LINK: auditory, visual
ORGANISATION: maths buddies
RESOURCES: 0–9 number cards; game grids (see below)

WHAT TO DO

● Players take two cards from a pile of 0–9 number cards.
● The two numbers shown are then multiplied together and players try to make one of the targets on the grid.
● For every target made, players score 7 points (or whatever multiple you like).
● The game ends after each player has had 12 throws.
● The winner is the player with the most points.
● Three games are played overall.

		Game	
Targets	**1**	**2**	**3**
Factor of 48	8 and 6		
Multiple of 5			
4 factors	3 x 5		
A square number			
Product < a score			
Product > 42			
Multiple of 8			
6 factors			
Both numbers factors of 12			
A prime number			
A composite number			

NOW TRY THIS

Invent your own targets for swap games with each other.

GOING LOOPY

OBJECTIVE: to improve ability to multiply by 2, 5 and 10
LEARNING LINK: auditory, visual, kinaesthetic
ORGANISATION: maths buddies
RESOURCES: loop cards (see below)

START 45	8 x 2	16	5 sets of 5
25	10 x 6	60	Double 9
18	5 lots of 6	30	8 x 10
80	Twice 7	14	8 x 5
40	10 times 10	100	2 x 6
12	5 times 4	20	4 lots of 2
8	1 lot of 5	5	5 x 10
50	Double 3	6	Twice 5
10	7 x 10	80	2 x 2
4	3 lots of 5	15	9 x 10
90	0 sets of 2	0	1 times 2
2	9 x 5		

WHAT TO DO

● Each child has a loop card (children can share or for some groups it may be appropriate for children to have two or more cards each)
● Check that you can read your card.
● The child holding the start card reads out the sum or number to the rest of the group.
● The cards follow a sequence where the answer to one card appears on another card.
● The cards form a loop. The activity is completed when the starter learner's card is reached again.
● Record the time taken for the game to be played.

NOW TRY THIS

Use a set of blank loop cards and develop a set of your own.

BEING PRODUCTIVE

OBJECTIVE: to multiply up to and including 6 × 6
LEARNING LINK: auditory, visual
ORGANISATION: maths buddies
RESOURCES: dice; non-standard dice (or sticky labels to go over standard dice)

WHAT TO DO

● Roll two dice and multiply the numbers together.
● Investigate how many different products you can make with two dice.
● Record your ideas in a table. The first three have been written in for you

	Product
1 x 1	1
1 x 2	2
1 x 3	3

● Which is the lowest/highest number you can make with two dice?
● Which products can be made using different numbers on a dice? For example what if the numbers on the dice were 5, 6, 7, 8, 9, 10?

NOW TRY THIS

Which products could be made with three ordinary dice?

NAPIER'S BONES

OBJECTIVE: to improve ability to multiply any number
LEARNING LINK: auditory, visual
ORGANISATION: maths buddies
RESOURCES: photocopiable page 63: Napier's bones for each child (photocopy onto card and cut out)

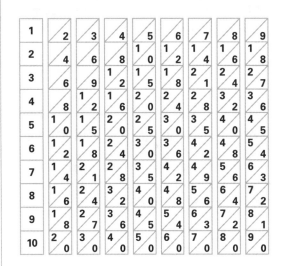

WHAT TO DO

● Each child has a set of 'Napier's bones'.
● Napier's bones are a set of sticks used to perform multiplication quickly. They were invented by the Scottish mathematician, John Napier.
● Each 'bone' is a list of the first nine multiples of a number between 1 and 9. There is an index bone for reference.
● Look at the times table patterns down each bone.
● How would you calculate 32 × 7?
● Lay out the two strips showing 3 and 2 at the top like this:

Line 1	3 2
Line 2	6 4
Line 3	9 6
Line 4	1/2 8
Line 5	1/5 1/0
Line 6	1/8 1/2
Line 7	2/1 1/4
Line 8	2/4 1/6
Line 9	2/7 1/8

To multiply this number by 7, add the numbers along the diagonals of the seventh line, starting at the right:

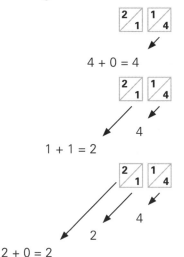

$$4 + 0 = 4$$
$$4$$
$$1 + 1 = 2$$
$$4$$
$$2$$
$$2 + 0 = 2$$

So the answer is 224.

Now try out some different numbers of your own.

NOW TRY THIS

After practising with one-digit numbers × two-digit numbers, practise using three- and four-digit numbers using 'Napier's bones'.

PRODUCT PITCH

OBJECTIVE: to improve ability to multiply any number
LEARNING LINK: visual, auditory
ORGANISATION: maths buddies
RESOURCES: football pitch gameboard (see below); two dice labelled 4, 5, 6, 7, 8, 9; counters

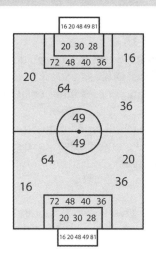

WHAT TO DO

- Choose a goal each and place your counter inside the net.
- The idea of the game is that you have to get from your goal to your opponent's goal to score.
- Take turns to roll the dice. Multiply the numbers together to make a product.
- If the number is in the next section of the pitch move forward; if it isn't then you stay where you are.
- To score a goal you must throw two numbers that multiply together to make 16, 24, 48, 49 or 81.
- The first player to score wins the game.

NOW TRY THIS

The numbers inside each section of the pitch can be changed, increased or decreased.

THAT'S MAGIC!

OBJECTIVE: to improve ability to multiply up to 10
LEARNING LINK: auditory, visual
ORGANISATION: maths buddies
RESOURCES: a pack of playing cards

WHAT TO DO

- Take out the tens and picture cards from a pack of playing cards.
- Shuffle the remaining cards well.
- Ask your buddy to select a card.
- Ask them to remember it and place it face down in front of them without showing you.

- Now give the following instructions:
  Multiply the number on the card by 2.
  Add 3 to the answer.
  Multiply this number by 5.
  If the card is a club, add 1.
  If the card is a diamond, add 2.
  If the card is a heart, add 3.
  If the card is a spade, add 4.
  Now subtract 15 from your answer.

This number tells you which card was originally chosen – the first digit is the card's value and the second digit tells you its suit (1 = clubs, 2 = diamonds, 3 = hearts, 4 = spades).

WHAT'S THE SCORE?

OBJECTIVE: to multiply up to 10
LEARNING LINK: auditory, visual
ORGANISATION: small groups
RESOURCES: lots of 1–6 dice

WHAT TO DO

- Play in two teams.
- The first player from each team throws two dice and multiplies the amounts shown.

Each team scores points as follows:
  Even numbers score 1 ½ points
  Odd numbers score 2 ½ points
  Multiples of 3 score 3 points
  Multiples of 4 score 4 points
  Multiples of 5 score 5 points
  Numbers with exactly six factors score 6 points

For example, if you threw a 5 and a 4, that would give a product of 20. 20 is an even number (1 ½ points), and it is a multiple of 4 (4 points) and a multiple of 5 (5 points), and it has exactly six factors (6 points), making a total of 16.5.

- The game is played five times. The winner is the player/team with the largest total after five rounds.

NOW TRY THIS

Change the number of dice thrown and the scoring system. For example, throw four dice to form two pairs, multiply and add the products. Use different multiples and score the maximum number of points if a prime number is made.

DIAMOND 9

OBJECTIVE: to improve ability to multiply any number

LEARNING LINK: visual, auditory

ORGANISATION: maths buddies

RESOURCES: Diamond 9 cards (see below) (or write these on the board and get children to write them on sticky notes); a fictitious Diamond 9 completed by a fictitious group with deliberate mistakes

WHAT TO DO

- Play in buddy pairs.
- Each pair is given a set of Diamond 9 cards with multiplication and division statements printed on them.

4 sets of 6	2 times 5
12 divided by 3	10 x 0
4 lots of 2 1/2	28 ÷ 7
Twice 12	100 ÷ 10
3 x 9	

- Rank each statement in order of value with the highest number at the top and the smallest number at the bottom. Place the other cards in between accordingly in the shape of a diamond. For example,

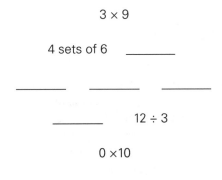

$$3 \times 9$$

4 sets of 6 _____

_____ _____ _____

_____ $12 \div 3$

0×10

- Join with another maths pair so that you can compare and contrast your diamonds and share ideas.
- Your teacher will give you a completed Diamond 9 completed by another group. Are the statements in the right order?
- Try the activity with a single times table or division table or a mixture of both.

NOW TRY THIS

Instead of a Diamond 9 you could use a Diamond 4 version to make it easier. Try a Diamond 12 to make it more challenging. Make a set of blank cards in a Diamond 9 and write your own version for another group to try.

CARD SORT

OBJECTIVE: to improve ability to multiply any number

LEARNING LINK: visual, auditory, kinaesthetic

ORGANISATION: maths trios or quads

RESOURCES: multiplication and division cards (see below)

WHAT TO DO

- Each group has a set of multiplication and division cards. Discuss your answers and place your cards into one of three columns: 'agree', 'disagree' or 'it depends on'.
- Discuss each decision with other groups.
- Focus on statements that you disagree on. Try to agree by testing out the statements through examples.

The product of two even numbers is always odd.	The square of an odd number is always odd.
The answer to a division sum is called the product.	An even number multiplied by an odd number gives an even quotient.
Even numbers can't be divided by 3.	The multiplier is always the smallest number in a multiplication sum.
Dividing two even numbers always makes an even quotient.	Divide is the inverse of multiply but multiply is not the inverse of divide.
A divisor is always the smallest number in a division sum.	If you square a number you always make it twice as big.
Division is the same as repeated addition.	Multiplying is easier than dividing.

NOW TRY THIS

Now create your own card sorts for other groups to consider. Focus on actual problems such as 4 ÷ 0.5 is greater than 7, 9 × 5 makes a square number, and so on.

ANSWERS	
False	True
False	True
False/It depends	True
False	False
True	False
False	False/It depends

TABLE CHALLENGE

OBJECTIVE: to improve ability to multiply any number
LEARNING LINK: visual, auditory
ORGANISATION: maths buddies
RESOURCES: number cards 1–10; two dice

WHAT TO DO

● Each pair has a set of 1–10 number cards and two dice.
● Shuffle the number cards and place them in a row face down.
● The first player chooses any card and turns it over to reveal the number.
● Roll both dice and add their total.
● Player one must give the answer (card number × dice total) within five seconds.
● If successful, keep the card. If not, turn it over again.
● Player two has a turn.
● The winner is the player with the most cards.

NOW TRY THIS

Adapt the game by increasing the number of cards and/or using more dice.

ROLL AND SPOT

OBJECTIVE: to improve ability to multiply any number
LEARNING LINK: visual, auditory
ORGANISATION: maths buddies
RESOURCES: two dice; product chart (see below)

WHAT TO DO

● With a maths buddy, roll two dice.
● For the first dice, square the score and then subtract 1.
● For the second die, double the score and subtract 1.
● Record this in the table below.

First dice (square and subtract 1)	Second dice (double and subtract 1)	Product

● Now multiply the two scores together to get the product.

● From your results, write in all the scores that can fit the statements written in the product chart below.

Product chart	
The product has four factors.	
The product is a multiple of 6.	
The product is divisible by 7.	
The product is an even number between 150 and 230.	
The product is divisible by 8.	
The product has a digital root of 3.	
The product is a multiple of 5.	

● Were there any statements that you couldn't find numbers for?

NOW TRY THIS

Create additional statements to investigate, for example, *The product is a prime number, The product with the greatest number of factors*, and so on.

BIG TIMES

OBJECTIVE: to improve ability to multiply any number
LEARNING LINK: visual, auditory
ORGANISATION: maths buddies
RESOURCES: dice; paper and pencils

WHAT TO DO

● Both of you draw a gameboard like this on your piece of paper.

● Take it in turns to throw a dice. Write the number thrown in any of the boxes on the gameboard.
● After four throws, each player's gameboard will show a four-digit number. For example, 1 x 2 x 3 x 4 = 24
● Each player then multiplies the numbers on their gameboard.
● The winner is the player with the largest product.

NOW TRY THIS

1. Play the same game but with just two cards and a two-digit number at the beginning.
2. Each player has one minute to rearrange their digits to make a larger product.
3. Players rearrange their digits to try to make the smallest product.

FACTOR THIS

OBJECTIVE: to improve ability to multiply and divide any number
LEARNING LINK: visual, auditory
ORGANISATION: maths buddies
RESOURCES: two dice labelled 1–6

WHAT TO DO

● Take turns to roll two dice to make a two-digit number, such as 26.
● Do this twice more so that each player has three two-digit numbers.
● Each player writes down all the factors of the numbers thrown.
● Players add all the factors together.
● The bigger total wins.

NOW TRY THIS

Use dice labelled 3, 4, 5, 6, 7, 8 and generate three or four-digit numbers.

FINGER FUN

OBJECTIVE: to improve ability to multiply any number
LEARNING LINK: visual, auditory
ORGANISATION: maths buddies
RESOURCES: none required

WHAT TO DO

● Ask your buddy to write the following numbers on your fingers and thumbs: 10 on each thumb, 9 on each index finger, 8 on each middle finger, 7 on each ring finger and 6 on each little finger.
● Swap over and write the same numbers on your buddy's fingers and thumbs.
● Now multiply two numbers together, for example 8 × 9 by following these steps:
Join the 8 finger on the left hand with the 9 finger on the right hand.
The two fingers that have just joined and any other fingers beneath them are worth 'ten'. So, in this case we have a value of 70. The fingers above those joined are now multiplied together. So, on your left hand you have two fingers above the join and on your right hand you have one finger above the join making 2 × 1.
Now add 70 and 2 to make 72.
Try this with other multiplications to test it out.

NOW TRY THIS

Have finger multiplication demonstrations between groups to show off how to solve multiplications.

SNAP SNAP

OBJECTIVE: to improve ability to divide any number
LEARNING LINK: visual, auditory
ORGANISATION: pairs or small groups
RESOURCES: a set of playing cards for each group

WHAT TO DO

● Divide the cards between you.
● Each player places a card and the cards are added together as they are played.
● When the total is a number divisible by 3, you call SNAP SNAP and the cards are won.

NOW TRY THIS

Change the rules so that SNAP SNAP is called when the total is divisible by another number.

SNAKES AND LADDERS

OBJECTIVE: to improve ability to multiply any number
LEARNING LINK: visual, auditory
ORGANISATION: pairs or small groups
RESOURCES: snakes and ladders playing board for each group; dice and counters

WHAT TO DO

● Roll the dice – the lowest number starts first.
● Take turns rolling a dice and move forward that number of spaces.
● If you land on a multiple of 6, move backwards two spaces. If you land on a multiple of 7, move forward two spaces. If you land on a square number, you miss a go.

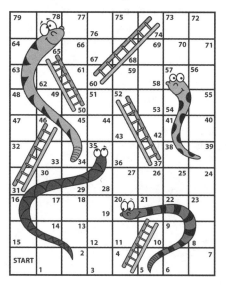

NOW TRY THIS

Change the rules so that landing on a different multiple equals a different penalty or reward.

FLAPPER

OBJECTIVE: to multiply by any number
LEARNING LINK: visual, auditory
ORGANISATION: maths buddies
RESOURCES: paper and pens

WHAT TO DO

● Create a flapper template as above. Place it on a flat surface with the writing facing down. The text in the middle should include a challenge under each number, such as, 'Count in threes in a dramatic voice' or 'Count in nines backwards from 81'.
● Fold back the four corners so that they touch in the middle.
● Turn over the flapper and fold back the corners so that they touch in the middle of the square.
● Now fold in half again.
● Put your right thumb and index finger in the right side and your left thumb and index finger in the left side. Open and close the flapper by moving your fingers.
● Take it in turns to play. Keep playing until you are familiar with the multiplication facts.

NOW TRY THIS

Make your own 'flapper' for another times table.

FLIPPER

OBJECTIVE: to multiply by any number
LEARNING LINK: visual, auditory
ORGANISATION: maths buddies
RESOURCES: decks of playing cards for each pair the following written on the board: Ace = 1, J = 0, Q = 11, K = 12

WHAT TO DO

● Shuffle a pack of playing cards. Deal them equally between you face down.
● Both players turn over one card from their pile at the same time.
● The first player to shout out the correct product wins both cards.

● Continue the game until all the cards have been turned over. The winner is the player with the most cards.

NOW TRY THIS

Try this game with division. After both cards have been flipped, roll a dice. Players have to divide the product by the number thrown. The first player to find the answer keeps both cards.

FACTOR FUN

OBJECTIVE: to multiply by any number
LEARNING LINK: visual, auditory
ORGANISATION: maths buddies
RESOURCES: factor boards (see below); dice

WHAT TO DO

● Each player has a copy of the factor board.
● Throw both dice to make a two-digit number. For example, a 4 and 2 could make 42 or 24.
● Write the number you have made in one of the boxes on your factor board
● You score 2 points if the number is a multiple of either numbers above and to the left of the space you choose.
● If it is a multiple of both, you score 4 points.
● For example, placing 42 as below would score two points because 42 is a multiple of 6 but not of 8. 14 would score four points because both 2 and 7 are multiples of 14.

	2	5	6	Score
7	14			
8			42	
3				
Score				

Total

● When all the spaces are filled, add the points scored for each row and column.
● The player with the highest total is the winner.

NOW TRY THIS

Use one dice and the following board. Score two points if the number thrown is a factor of either of the numbers above and to the left of that space. If it is a factor of both numbers, you score six points.

	20	35	18	Score
24				
10				
36				
Score				

Total

TAKE COVER

OBJECTIVE: to improve ability to multiply by any number

LEARNING LINK: visual, auditory

ORGANISATION: maths buddies

RESOURCES: number board (see below); dice; counters

WHAT TO DO

● Take turns to roll the dice to make a number. For example, throwing a 2 and a 3 could be 23 or 32.

● Now find two factors of this number on the number board and cover them with your counters.

● For example, if the number is 32, a pair of factors could be 8 and 4.

● The aim of the game is to get four factors in a line.

7	11	3	12	2	9	5
11	6	4	3	7	4	2
8	9	7	3	6	5	12
6	2	4	8	3	5	11
8	5	12	9	2	9	4
4	5	12	7	3	6	8
3	2	5	7	8	9	2

NOW TRY THIS

Increase or decrease the grid size. Play as a competition as a whole class.

AMAZING MULTIPLES

OBJECTIVE: to improve ability to multiply by any number

LEARNING LINK: visual, auditory

ORGANISATION: maths buddies

RESOURCES: maze boards (see below); counters

WHAT TO DO

● Look at the maze boards. Find the start and finish boxes.

● Now find a way through the maze from start (S) to finish (F) by following a trail.

● In the first trail, you have to follow multiples of 3. In the second trail, you have to follow multiples of 4.

● Use counters of the same colour to mark your way through the numbers.

● You can only move one square at a time horizontally, vertically or diagonally.

S
12	2	36	6	64	4	19	91	56	26	47	19	27
31	27	49	8	33	13	34	21	25	58	50	18	16
4	11	20	15	65	10	66	38	81	14	3	103	105
17	56	42	16	29	51	88	40	55	108	16	42	2
50	100	89	9	24	7	22	76	113	24	62	49	99

F

S
14	32	12	12	84	58	26	77	4	50	2	87
16	34	8	46	94	66	19	23	16	13	21	104
24	54	14	25	11	20	128	86	114	46	36	28
45	52	101	4	64	43	78	28	54	16	72	14
28	41	76	26	55	92	13	12	56	45	34	144

F

NOW TRY THIS

Choose another multiple. Have a go at making your own multiple trail.

FACTOR POINT

OBJECTIVE: to improve ability to multiply by any number

LEARNING LINK: visual, auditory

ORGANISATION: maths buddies

RESOURCES: a pack of playing cards; Ace = 1, J = 0, Q = 11, K = 12 written on the board

WHAT TO DO

● Shuffle the cards. Deal them face down in five rows of ten – there should be two left over – these are example cards.

● Multiply the two cards left over and then work out how many factors the product has.

● If the product has two factors then score two points, three factors scores three points, and so on.

● Now take it in turns to take any two cards and keep playing until there are no more cards left.

● Keep a running total of the factors scored.

● The winner is the player with the most factor points.

NOW TRY THIS

Award extra points for any player who makes a prime number, a number with nine factors or a square number.

WHAT A CARD

OBJECTIVE: to improve ability to multiply by any number

LEARNING LINK: visual, auditory

ORGANISATION: maths buddies

RESOURCES: a pack of playing cards; a number board for each pair (see below); Ace = 1, J = 0, Q = 11, K = 12 written on the board

54	35	100
36	7	24
63	56	28
12	27	30

WHAT TO DO

● Shuffle the cards and place them in a pile in front of you.

● Take it in turns to turn over two cards.

● If they multiply together to make one of the numbers above, score that number of points and keep the cards.

● If they don't make one of the numbers in the number box, put them in a discard pile.

● The game ends when all cards have been turned over.

● The winner is the player with the most points when added up.

NOW TRY THIS

Make the number box board bigger and use different numbers as the target numbers.

FIVES AND THREES

OBJECTIVE: to improve ability to divide any number

LEARNING LINK: visual, auditory

ORGANISATION: maths buddies

RESOURCES: standard set of dominoes (28 tiles) per pair; pencils and paper

WHAT TO DO

● Each player takes six dominoes.

● Dominoes are played so that the touching ends match in number.

● If a player cannot go then he/she 'knocks'.

● If the sum of the exposed ends of the line of dominoes adds up to a multiple of 5 and/or 3, the player scores a number of points based on that multiple. For example, if the exposed ends of the line of dominoes add up to 10, the player scores two points because $10 \div 5 = 2$.

● If the end total is 15, this scores 8 because $15 \div 5 = 3$ and $15 \div 3 = 5$, so $3 + 5 = 8$.

● Continuing playing until a player uses all his/her dominoes, or no player can lay any more dominoes. The player who finished, or the player with the least total number of spots remaining scores one additional point.

● Shuffle the dominoes again and each player draws six for the next round.

● Continue the game until a player reaches 51 exactly. If a player is on 50 points and scores two points, then those points don't count. He/she has to gain one point to finish on 51 exactly.

NOW TRY THIS

Change the rules so that the winning number is 101.

THROW AND CROSS

OBJECTIVE: to improve ability to multiply by any number

LEARNING LINK: visual, auditory

ORGANISATION: maths buddies

RESOURCES: dice; pencils and paper

WHAT TO DO

● Throw five dice and write down the numbers thrown.

● Now cross out any twos and fours.

● Multiply the numbers you are left with. For example, if you threw 5, 6, 4, 3, and 2, you would cross out the 4 and 2 and be left with 5, 6 and 3. Multiplying these together, $5 \times 6 \times 3$, makes 90. Remove the dice that produced the 4 and 2.

● Throw the remaining dice again – if you throw any twos or fours, cross them out and remove the dice. Multiply the numbers you have left and add this to the number you made on your last go. For example, if you threw 5, 1, 2, you would times 5 and 1 to make 5 and add this to 90 to make 95.

● Keep playing until you are left with just one number. The winner is the player with the highest score.

NOW TRY THIS

This game can be complicated by adding one more dice. Rather than crossing out twos and fours, you could cross out ones and threes. You could change the numbers on the dice to 3, 4, 5, 6, 7, 8

MULTI-TRIO

OBJECTIVE: to improve ability to multiply by any number

LEARNING LINK: visual, auditory

ORGANISATION: groups of three

RESOURCES: a pack of playing cards; coloured counters; playing board (see below); Ace = 1, J = 0, Q = 11, K = 12 written on the board

WHAT TO DO

● Shuffle the cards and place them in a pile next to the playing board.

● Take it in turns to select two cards.

● Multiply the numbers together. If the product made is on the grid, cover that number with a coloured counter.

● The first player to get three counters in a row is the winner.

42	50	45	36	16	48	27	35
56	9	40	28	20	18	30	32
60	48	12	3	24	36	3	12
32	7	45	36	8	49	54	10
35	15	18	9	6	100	64	81
56	54	2	28	1	9	16	25
121	90	40	72	63	64	60	18
21	20	16	14	80	55	66	25

NOW TRY THIS

Instead of three in a line, aim to cover four in a diagonal line.

GOTCHA!

OBJECTIVE: to improve ability to multiply by any number

LEARNING LINK: visual, auditory

ORGANISATION: groups of four

RESOURCES: a pack of playing cards; Ace = 1, J = 0, Q = 11, K = 12 written on the board; two dice labelled 3, 4, 5, 6, 7 and 8

WHAT TO DO

● Deal out seven cards to each player.

● Now roll the two dice.

● Players multiply the two numbers together and call *Gotcha!* if they have two numbers in their hand that equal that product.

● The dealer checks the multiplications and the game continues.

● The winner is the player who is left with one card which is a factor of the two dice thrown when multiplied.

NOW TRY THIS

Change the value of the picture cards to make the game harder.

LUCK OF THE DRAW

OBJECTIVE: to improve ability to multiply by any number

LEARNING LINK: visual, auditory

ORGANISATION: maths buddies

RESOURCES: a pack of playing cards; Ace = 1, J = 0, Q = 11, K = 12 written on the board

WHAT TO DO

● Shuffle a pack of playing cards.

● Now deal out two cards each.

● If the cards multiply together to make a number in the six- or seven-times tables, score three points. If they multiply together to make a number in the eight- or nine-times tables, score five points. Any other tables score no points.

● Keep a running total of the points you score.

● Play continues until all the cards in the pile run out.

● The player with the most points wins.

NOW TRY THIS

Adapt the points system so that points are scored for only other times tables, or so that any odd product made scores one point.

ON YOUR MARKS

OBJECTIVE: to improve ability to multiply any number
LEARNING LINK: visual, auditory
ORGANISATION: groups of four
RESOURCES: race board (see below); counters; dice

WHAT TO DO
- Each group has a race board.
- Each player selects a number (or 'runner') on the starting line.
- Players take turns to roll the two dice. These are multiplied together to get a product (a runner).
- The player or runner whose number is the same product can move one square using one of the counters.
- Play the game and see which number finishes first.
- Repeat the game a few times.
- Does the same runner always win?
- Is the game fair?
- Which runner is most likely/least likely to win?

										Finish
1										
2										
3										
4										
5										
6										
9										
12										
15										
16										
18										
20										
24										
25										
30										
36										

NOW TRY THIS
Try using different numbers on the dice and change the runners on the race board.

FIRST PAST THE POST

OBJECTIVE: to improve ability to multiply any number
LEARNING LINK: visual, auditory
ORGANISATION: maths buddies
RESOURCES: dice (labelled 3, 4, 5, 6, 7, 8); score sheet (see below)

WHAT TO DO
- Throw the two dice.
- Multiply the numbers thrown and find the product – this is your score.
- Record your throw and product on the score sheet.
- Take it in turns to keep throwing the dice.
- Both keep a check on the products.
- Keep a running total score after every go.

For example:

Player 1

Dice thrown	Product score	Total
6 and 7	42	42
3 and 8	24	66

Player 2

Dice thrown	Product score	Total
6 and 6	36	36
8 and 5	40	76

- The first player to reach 201 or more is the winner.

NOW TRY THIS
Change the target total or use different target dice such as 2, 3, 4, 5, 6 and 7 on one dice and 5, 6, 7, 8, 9 and 10 on the other.

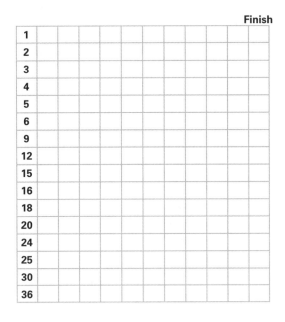

GOESINTA

OBJECTIVE: to improve ability to divide any number
LEARNING LINK: visual, auditory
ORGANISATION: maths buddies
RESOURCES: dice (labelled 2, 3, 4, 5, 6 and 7); coloured counters; number board

WHAT TO DO

- Each pair has a number board.
- Take turns to throw the dice.
- If this number can go into a number on the board exactly, without a remainder, then place a counter on top of the number.

56	63	48	15	30
27	28	35	36	20
49	18	81	40	72
42	21	4	84	58
30	64	10	7	22

- You cannot place a counter on a number that has already been covered.
- The winner is the player who has covered the most numbers after all the numbers have been covered.

NOW TRY THIS

Change the numbers on both dice and the board.

ANTICLOCKWISE

OBJECTIVE: to improve ability to divide any number
LEARNING LINK: visual, auditory
ORGANISATION: maths buddies
RESOURCES: two dice, one labelled 1–6 and the other labelled 6, 7, 8, 9, 10 and 11; coloured counters; clock face (see below)

WHAT TO DO

- Take turns to throw the dice.
- Divide the number on the larger dice by the number on the smaller dice.

- If there is a remainder then move your counter that number of spaces anticlockwise round the clock.
- If there is no remainder then don't move.
- If a number is occupied, another counter cannot land on that number and so the player misses a go.
- When each player reaches number 1 going anticlockwise play continues, but any future moves go clockwise.
- The winner is the player who ends back at number 12.

NOW TRY THIS

Try using different numbers on the dice to make this game more challenging.

MOVE IT

OBJECTIVE: to improve ability to multiply and divide any number
LEARNING LINK: visual, auditory
ORGANISATION: maths buddies
RESOURCES: three dice labelled 3, 4, 5, 6, 7 and 8; photocopiable page 59: Hundred square; different-coloured counters

WHAT TO DO

- Take turns to throw two dice and multiply them together.
- Now roll the third dice. Divide the product made from the last throw by this number.
- If there is a remainder, this is the number of spaces you move forward.
- If you land on a square number (except for 100), you miss a go (1, 4, 9, 16, 25, 36, 49, 64, 81).
- The winner is the first player to land on or beyond 100.

1	2	3	4	5	6	7	8	9	10
11	12	13	14	15	16	17	18	19	20
21	22	23	24	25	26	27	28	29	30
31	32	33	34	35	36	37	38	39	40
41	42	43	44	45	46	47	48	49	50
51	52	53	54	55	56	57	58	59	60
61	62	63	64	65	66	67	68	69	70
71	72	73	74	75	76	77	78	79	80
81	82	83	84	85	86	87	88	89	90
91	92	93	94	95	96	97	98	99	100

NOW TRY THIS

Add another rule. If you land on any multiple of 8, then have another go.

PRODUCT GRID

OBJECTIVE: to improve ability to multiply and divide any number

LEARNING LINK: visual, auditory

ORGANISATION: whole class

RESOURCES: one dice labelled 1, 2, 3, 4, 5 and 6

WHAT TO DO

● Each player draws a grid like this.

	36	24	48	Score
6				
20				
30				
Score				

● The dice is thrown. Each player places the number thrown in one of the nine spaces.

● Do this until all the spaces have been filled.

● Once a number has been placed in a square, it cannot be moved.

● Players score one point for each time a row or column is the product of the three numbers in that row or column. The bottom right-hand corner is for totalling scores.

● For example:

	36	24	48	Score
6	4	4	6	0
20	2	3	2	0
30	5	2	3	1
Score	0	1	0	2

● The player with the highest score wins.

● Play several times.

NOW TRY THIS

Try the game with different number headings.

PYRAMID POWER

OBJECTIVE: to improve ability to multiply and divide any number

LEARNING LINK: visual, auditory

ORGANISATION: whole class

RESOURCES: number cards 1, 2, 4, 6, 8 and 12

WHAT TO DO

● Move the number cards around in the shape of a pyramid so that the product of the three numbers on each side makes 48.

● The cards are set out as follows:

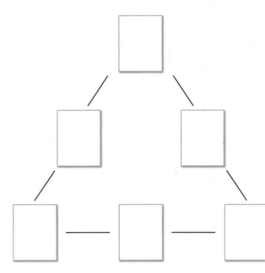

NOW TRY THIS

Find more than one way of solving the problem. What do you notice?

> **ANSWER**
> The 1, 4 and 6 have to go in the corners.

501

OBJECTIVE: to improve ability to multiply and divide any number

LEARNING LINK: visual, auditory

ORGANISATION: whole class

RESOURCES: two dice labelled 3, 4, 5, 6, 7 and 8

WHAT TO DO

● Take it in turns to roll two dice.

● Write down the product of the numbers.

● When it is your turn again, the result is added to your previous product.

● Continue play and keep a running total.

● The winner is the player who makes exactly 501.

● If you go over 501, you miss your next go.

NOW TRY THIS

Use dice labelled 1–6 and aim to reach 101.

KINAESTHETIC LEARNING

Multiples of 3	Multiples of 4	Multiples of 3	Multiples of 4

Digit cards	Digit cards
Children	Children

VENN RACE

OBJECTIVE: to improve ability to multiply any number
LEARNING LINK: tactile, auditory
ORGANISATION: maths buddies
RESOURCES: large hoops; number cards 0–25; rope/cone

WHAT TO DO

- The class is divided into several teams.
- Each team has two hoops placed side by side with an overlap at one end of the hall. Children stand at the other end behind a rope line or cone.
- Each child has a number card from 0–25, which are placed in a pile in front of the team.
- You need to place all the multiples of 3 in the left-hand hoop and all the multiples of 4 in the right-hand hoop.
- Place the cards in a relay race. One child turns over a card, runs up to the hula hoops, places it where they think it should go, and runs back to tag a team member who does the same, and so on, until all the cards have been placed.
- Remember: any numbers that are multiples of both 3 and 4 go in the overlap.
- Numbers that do not 'live' inside the hoops are placed outside of the hoops.
- The first team to complete their Venn diagram scores 12 points, second place scores 6 points and third place scores 3 points. Other teams score zero.
- When all teams have completed their Venn diagrams, check the circles for accurate number placement and score 10 points for all numbers correctly placed. The winning team is the team with the most points.
- What is special about the numbers in the overlap? Make sure that you understand that these are common multiples.

NOW TRY THIS

Investigate other number combinations, for example 2 and 4, 3 and 5, 6 and 7. Then move on to looking at three circles and investigating the multiples of three numbers.

RHYTHMATHS

OBJECTIVE: to improve ability to multiply any number
LEARNING LINK: tactile, auditory
ORGANISATION: whole class
RESOURCES: large space

WHAT TO DO:

- Everyone sits in a circle.
- One child leads the game by starting a rhythmic sequence using body percussion. For example, two thigh slaps and two hand claps.
- The rest of the class joins in with the pattern.
- When the pattern is established, your teacher will state a multiplication fact during the thigh slapping stage.
- Join in with the next multiplication fact from that times table with the next two thigh slaps.
- The pattern continues until the times table is complete.

NOW TRY THIS

Play with each child in turn saying the answer to a multiplication fact. If someone cannot answer they drop out of the rhythm and play carries on to the next child. The last child left is the winner.

RUBBISH NUMBERS

OBJECTIVE: to improve ability to multiply any number
LEARNING LINK: tactile, auditory, visual
ORGANISATION: groups of three or four
RESOURCES: four labelled cardboard boxes for each group; one pack of 1–25 number cards for each group

DUSTBIN A MULTIPLES OF 4

DUSTBIN B MULTIPLES OF 5

DUSTBIN C MULTIPLES OF 6

DUSTBIN D OTHER NUMBERS

WHAT TO DO:

● You have been given the job of sorting through a big pile of numbers for recycling.
● There are four empty boxes (number dustbins) per group at one end of the hall. Groups stand in a line at the other end of the hall.
● Shuffle a pack of 1–25 number cards and place them in front of you.
● The first player in your group turns over the card and runs to the end of the hall to place the number in the correct box, then runs back to tag the next player.
● Play continues until all the numbers have been placed.
● The winners are the group who place the most numbers in the dustbins correctly.

NOW TRY THIS

1. Can you add some numbers to the list for another group to sort? Try inventing your own 'Rubbish numbers' game using different groups and numbers.
2. You can also play this game by your teacher drawing some completed number dustbins on the board that deliberately contain some misplaced numbers. Group members consult with each other to agree on which numbers need moving to another dustbin.

DASH AND TAG

OBJECTIVE: to improve ability to multiply by any number
LEARNING LINK: visual, auditory
ORGANISATION: whole class
RESOURCES: multiplication flash cards

WHAT TO DO

● The class is divided into two groups. Both groups line up in two lines on one side of the hall.
● There are two equal stacks of multiplication flash cards on the opposite side of the hall.
● At the blow of a whistle, the first person in one line races to the other side of the hall and picks up a card from the pile of cards and answers the question to your teacher.
● If the answer is correct, the card is given to your teacher and the player then races to tag the next person in line.
● If a player does not know the answer or gives the wrong answer, he or she puts the card on the bottom of the pile and selects the next card. The player then keeps selecting cards until he or she knows the answer to one of them.
● When the cards run out the other team starts their turn.
● The first team to correctly give the answer to all the multiplication facts in its pile wins.

NOW TRY THIS

1. Try mixing multiplication and division facts in the game.
2. Try playing in smaller groups.

PLATE FRENZY

OBJECTIVE: to improve ability to multiply by any number
LEARNING LINK: visual, auditory, tactile
ORGANISATION: groups of four or five
RESOURCES: multiplication flash cards; paper plates (write the multiples of 7 on the face of 12 paper plates. Now write 20 numbers that aren't in the seven-times table on 20 other plates)

WHAT TO DO
● There are lots of paper plates face down all around the hall.
● In your group, take it in turns to turn over a plate. Collect all the multiples of 7 as quickly as you can.
● After each group have collected the multiple of 7 plates, ask your teacher how long you took.
● The plates will be replaced face down again. Play again.
● The group with the quickest time wins.

NOW TRY THIS
1. Try this game with different multiples.
2. Play so that when a team have collected the plates, they have to say the times table being practised as a group.

STEPPING STONES

OBJECTIVE: to improve ability to multiply by any number
LEARNING LINK: visual, auditory, tactile
ORGANISATION: whole class
RESOURCES: 13 sheets of A4 paper; foam dice; photocopiable sheet 60: Factor sheet

WHAT TO DO
● Listen to the following tale:

A rich queen used to play games with her people. Each person who dared to play had a chance of winning a bag of gold coins. The queen had a staircase with 13 steps. The person started on the middle step, which meant that there were six steps up to the top where the bag of coins waited, and six steps down to a door which led to a dungeon. The queen tossed two dice (labelled 3, 4, 5, 6, 7 and 8). The rules were as follows:
If the product of the numbers on the two dice is an even number and bigger than 2, move one step up.

If the product of the numbers on the two dice is a prime number, move down 2 steps. If the product has exactly four factors, move up four steps.

● There are 13 sheets of A4 paper across the floor. One child stands on the middle 'step'.
● Another child throws two large foam dice. The child on the step must multiply the numbers thrown.
● Look at the rules to see whether they move closer to the gold or closer to the dungeon.
● The game is played until the top step or bottom step is reached.
● Another child has a go.

NOW TRY THIS
The game can be played by changing the number or steps or the rules. For example, if you make a square number then move back two spaces, and so on.

RACE TO 200

OBJECTIVE: to improve ability to multiply by any number
LEARNING LINK: visual, auditory, tactile
ORGANISATION: two teams of three
RESOURCES: sets of dominoes; four dice

WHAT TO DO
● Teams sit two tables away from the board but with a clear path to the board so that they can run safely to it.
● Mix the dominoes. Both teams take 14 dominoes each and turn them face down. Teams also need two dice each.
● One player from each team rolls the dice, multiplying the two numbers thrown and running to the board to write the product.
● This player then runs back to tag another player who turns over a domino, multiplies and runs to the board to add this product to the last number.
● This player runs back to tag the next player, who throws the dice and repeats the process.
● Keep repeating until one team scores 200 or more.
● Make sure you do not turn over dominoes too soon. Make sure that your multiplication and addition is correct!

NOW TRY THIS
Increase the target total or use differently numbered dice.

DIGITS UP

OBJECTIVE: to improve ability to multiply by any number
LEARNING LINK: visual, auditory
ORGANISATION: whole class
RESOURCES: none required

WHAT TO DO

● The class starts counting from 1.
● Each time a multiple of 6 is reached, put up your left hand.
● Continue counting and when a multiple of 7 is reached, put up your right hand.
● Put up both hands if the number is a multiple of both 6 and 7.
● If anyone makes a mistake, the count has to start again!

NOW TRY THIS

1. Rather than counting as a class, this game can be played individually, counting round the class.
2. Alter the multiples according to what you want to practise.
3. Children stand up on a multiple of 6 and raise both hands in the air and shake them on a multiple of 7.

> **ANSWER**
> Numbers that are multiples of both 6 and 7: 42, 84, 126, 168…

SPLAT!

OBJECTIVE: to recognise division and multiplication vocabulary
LEARNING LINK: visual, auditory, tactile
ORGANISATION: groups of three of four
RESOURCES: word labels (see list of words below); Blu-Tack®; coloured sticky notes – a different colour for each group (stick these around the hall in places that are easy to get to); definitions (see below)

WHAT TO DO

● The following words are around the hall in places that are easy to get to:

multiplicand, common factor, composite number, dividend, divisor, division, multiplication, quotient, product, factor, multiple

● Each group has some coloured sticky notes in a different colour.

● One of the definitions below will be called out:

> *The name given to the number that is being multiplied by another number.*
> *One quantity that is a factor of two or more other numbers.*
> *A number with more than two factors.*
> *The number that is divided by another number.*
> *The number that divides another number.*
> *The inverse of multiplication.*
> *The inverse of division.*
> *The answer to a division sum.*
> *The answer to a multiplication sum.*
> *A number that divides another number exactly.*
> *The product of a given number with another factor.*

● Discuss your ideas about the first definition. Which definition matches which word stuck around the hall?
● Select a runner. The runner then splats their sticky notes to the appropriate word.
● Runners return to their places
● Repeat with other definitions.
● If other groups have stuck their sticky notes on different words, explore these differences and try to reach an agreement.

NOW TRY THIS

Rather than use words and their definitions, you could play this game with multiplication and division sums and their products and quotients

> **ANSWERS**
> multiplicand
> common factor
> composite number
> dividend
> divisor
> division
> multiplication
> quotient
> product
> factor
> multiple

SCRAMBLE!

OBJECTIVE: to improve ability to multiply and divide any number

LEARNING LINK: visual, auditory, tactile

ORGANISATION: groups of four

RESOURCES: sum cards cut out (see below); hoops; labels

WHAT TO DO

● Three hoops are laid out in the classroom, hall or playground.

● One hoop is labelled '4 factors or less', another hoop '5 factors' and the other hoop '6 or more factors'.

● Turn your sum cards over one at a time. Place them inside one of the hoops. Once a card has been placed it cannot be moved.

$$36 \div 6$$
$$24 \div 3$$
$$144 \div 12$$
$$2 \times 8$$
$$7 \times 4$$
$$9 \times 9$$

● The team to place all cards correctly are the winners.

NOW TRY THIS

Try this game for a different set of numbers and different factors.

LINE UP

OBJECTIVE: to improve ability to multiply and divide any number

LEARNING LINK: visual, auditory, tactile

ORGANISATION: groups of seven or eight

RESOURCES: sticky labels showing numbers taken from the six-, seven-, eight- and nine-times tables; masking tape

WHAT TO DO

● There is a line of masking tape in four different places in the hall,

● Stand on any of the lines – only seven or eight children per line.

● You will be given a sticky label with a number on it. Place this on your jumper.

● When you are standing on one of the lines, your teacher will tell you what line you are standing on, for example, *This is the × 6 line, This is the ×7 line,* and so on.

● On the sound of a whistle, race to the line that matches your number, for example 49 would race to the × 7 line. Some numbers will be able to stand on more than one line, for example 24.

● All numbers on a line then have to stand in order.

NOW TRY THIS

Practise this game using different times tables and alter the number of people allowed on a line.

RUNAROUND

OBJECTIVE: to improve ability to multiply any number

LEARNING LINK: visual, auditory, tactile

ORGANISATION: groups of seven or eight

RESOURCES: sticky labels showing some numbers taken from the six-, seven-, eight- and nine-times tables

WHAT TO DO

● Place the sticky labels on your jumpers.

● Listen to the music and run around the hall.

● When the music stops, everyone freezes and listens for their times table call.

● If your teacher says 'Sixes move it!' then everyone with a number in the six-times table races to the front of the hall, stands in a line and calls out the six-times table together.

● When the music starts again, children run around and wait for the music to stop.

● Repeat for a different times table.

NOW TRY THIS

You could play this game in a north, east, south, west formation. For example, the six-times table are north, seven-times table are east, and so on. When the music stops, your teacher calls out *Go!* and you race to either north, east, south or west. Groups then take it in turns to say their tables.

ON THE MARCH

OBJECTIVE: to improve ability to multiply any number
LEARNING LINK: visual, auditory
ORGANISATION: whole class
RESOURCES: none required

WHAT TO DO

● Go out on to the playground and form yourselves into four columns of seven or eight children, facing your teacher.

● Each line is a group of multiplication soldiers.

● Your teacher will take you on a quick march across the playground chanting your chosen times table for you to repeat. You could say these in a US Marine style. For example:

> *1 times 7 that makes 7*
> *1 times 7 that makes 7*
>
> *2 lots of 7 make 14*
> *2 lots of 7 make 14*
>
> *21 comes from 7 × 3*
> *21 comes from 7 × 3*

And so on.

NOW TRY THIS

Each column of multiplication soldiers could march on the spot repeating a set of numbers in quick succession. For example, your teacher calls out *6, 12, 18, 24* which the line then repeats while marching in time to the chant. When you have gained some fluency, chant the tables backwards.

CHEERLEADER MATHS

OBJECTIVE: to improve ability to multiply any number
LEARNING LINK: visual, auditory
ORGANISATION: groups of five or six
RESOURCES: none required

WHAT TO DO

● Get into groups of five or six.

● Choreograph and chant a times table in the style of cheerleaders.

For example,

> *Give me a 6*
> *Give me 4*
> *What have you got?*
> *24*
> *I said 'What have you got?'*
> *We said 24!!*
>
> *Give me a 9*
> *Give me 6*
> *What have we got?*
> *We've got 54!*

And so on.

Challenge groups of children to team up to combine their cheers.

NOW TRY THIS

● Have a demonstration of all the group's chants and movements.

● When you have practised, hold a multiplication cheerleading competition.

MULTIPLE MADNESS

OBJECTIVE: to improve ability to multiply any number
LEARNING LINK: visual, auditory, tactile
ORGANISATION: groups of four
RESOURCES: none required

WHAT TO DO

● Get into groups of four.

● Invent a set of movements for a particular times table.

● For example, you could stand on one leg, jump, clap hands and so on, and say the appropriate times table as you perform the movement. All movements need to be different.

> *1 × 7 = stand on one leg*
> *2 × 7 = hop*
> *3 × 7 = lay face down*
> *4 × 7 = lay face up*
> *5 × 7 = point to the ceiling with both arms*

● After you have created your moves, these can then be performed to the rest of the class

NOW TRY THIS

Swap groups and learn another sequence with a different group, or perform the same times table and come up with different movements.

BODY BOP

OBJECTIVE: to improve ability to multiply any number
LEARNING LINK: visual, auditory, tactile
ORGANISATION: whole class
RESOURCES: none required

WHAT TO DO

- Stand up and mirror your teacher's actions.
- Choose a times table you want to practise, for example, the six-times table.
- Touch your left foot and say 6, right foot and say 12, left knee, 18, right knee, 24, left thigh slap, 30, right thigh slap, 36.
- Now start again but repeat the movements and chant to make it a little quicker.
- Start again and after 36, touch your left elbow with your right hand and say 42, left hand touches right elbow and say 48.
- Then it's left hand touch left ear lobe, 54, right hand right ear lobe, 60.
- Left eye wink, 66, right eye wink, 72.
- This works best when done at speed.

NOW TRY THIS

Repeat the actions but do them backwards.

HURRAY ARRAY

OBJECTIVE: to improve ability to multiply any number
LEARNING LINK: visual, auditory
ORGANISATION: whole class
RESOURCES: none required

WHAT TO DO

- Your teacher will shout out a number. You have to stand in a number array that matches that number. For example, the number 12 would result in a three groups of four arrangement or four groups of three. The number 20 could result in four groups of five or five groups of four.
- Suggest numbers for your friends to try.

NOW TRY THIS

Practise showing numbers in different group formations in a string of numbers. For example, you could learn the formations of five or six different numbers which you can arrange yourselves into one after the other.

SCISSORS, STONE, PAPER

OBJECTIVE: to improve ability to multiply any number
LEARNING LINK: visual, auditory, tactile
ORGANISATION: whole class
RESOURCES: none required

WHAT TO DO

- This is a game for three people.
- Two players face each other, each with one fist in full view. One person acts as a referee and problem setter.
- Players then both thump their fists up and down three times and then make one of the symbols below:
  Scissors – index finger and third fingers extended
  Stone – clenched fist
  Paper – flat hand

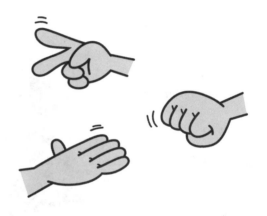

- The winner of each round is the one whose symbol 'overcomes' the other child's symbol: so scissors cut paper but are broken by stone; stone breaks scissors but can be wrapped in paper; paper can wrap stone, but is cut by scissors. If both of you show the same symbol, then it is a tie.
- The winner scores three points for every victory but can also score a bonus two points. After each win, the referee asks the winner a multiplication sum – if it is answered correctly, the bonus points are awarded. If it is answered incorrectly, the points go to the other player. The referee can check using a multiplication square.
- The referee keeps score. After an agreed score has been reached, players take turns to be the referee.

NOW TRY THIS

A number value could be assigned to the symbols so that scissors = 8×7, stone = 9×7 and paper = 6×7. Players overcome each other by saying whether their product is bigger than the other player's product.

BOXED NUMBERS

OBJECTIVE: to improve ability to multiply any number
LEARNING LINK: visual, auditory, tactile
ORGANISATION: groups of four
RESOURCES: 12 boxes (shoe boxes or similar) at one end of the hall labelled from 1–12 and containing the numbers from a times table that you are practising

WHAT TO DO

● Inside each box, there is a number from one of the tables you are practising. For example, if you are practising the eight times table then the numbers from 1 × 8 up to 12 × 8 will each be in one of the boxes but in the wrong order.
● Take it in turns in groups of four to race up to the boxes, look inside and place the numbers in the correct boxes.
● Each group will be timed.
● The winners are the group who get the numbers in the right boxes and in the fastest time.

NOW TRY THIS

Line the boxes up in the wrong order so that you have to place them in the right sequence too.

SKIP TO IT

OBJECTIVE: to improve ability to multiply any number
LEARNING LINK: visual, auditory, tactile
ORGANISATION: groups of three
RESOURCES: skipping ropes

WHAT TO DO

● Work in groups of three.
● Two children hold one end of rope each. The other child stands in the middle ready to jump.

● The rope is then swung. The person in the middle counts out a times table up to the 12th multiple. Two points are given for every jump made without touching the rope.
● Take it in turns. When everyone has had a go, repeat the round again.
● For any jump missed, a penalty of minus two points is given.

NOW TRY THIS

Say a times table forwards then backwards.

MULTIPLE CORNER

OBJECTIVE: to improve ability to multiply any number
LEARNING LINK: visual, auditory, tactile
ORGANISATION: whole class
RESOURCES: none required

WHAT TO DO

● Each corner of the hall is a times table. For example, one corner is the multiple of 6 corner, another is the multiple of 7 corner, another the multiple of 8 and the other corner is the multiple of 9 corner.
● Move around the hall in any way you want, dodging everyone else. Listen out for a number.
● Your teacher will call out a number from one of the times tables, such as 45. Run to the multiple corner that the number belongs to.
● When you have identified the correct multiple, everyone calls back: $45 \div 9 = 5$, $9 \times 5 = 45$
● Move around the hall listening for other numbers.
● Remember: your teacher may call out numbers that are not in any of the corners.

NOW TRY THIS

Try the game with your teacher calling out numbers for boys and girls separately.

X FACTOR

OBJECTIVE: to improve ability to multiply any number
LEARNING LINK: visual, auditory, tactile
ORGANISATION: small groups
RESOURCES: hoops; 0–9 number cards

WHAT TO DO

- Each group has some 0–9 cards
- Lay out some hoops at one end of the hall, one per group.
- Your teacher will call out a number. Each group has to decide how many factors that number has.
- Once you have made a decision, someone from your group runs to the hoop and puts the number inside. For example, if 25 was called out, the correct number to place in the hoop would be the number card 3, because 25 has 3 factors
- Every group placing a number correctly scores the number placed inside the hoop.
- Repeat this a number of times so that everyone has a turn at placing a number
- The winners are the group with the highest number of points after so many turns.

NOW TRY THIS

Try having two numbers called at the same time, for example 24 and 32, and place two numbers in the hoops.

PLACE ME

OBJECTIVE: to improve ability to multiply any number
LEARNING LINK: visual, auditory, tactile
ORGANISATION: small groups
RESOURCES: hoops; 0–9 number cards

WHAT TO DO

- Each group has a hoop placed at one end of the hall and two sets of 0–9 cards each.

- Your teacher will call out a product. Run to the hoop and place two numbers from your set of 0–9 cards that multiply together to make that product.
- For example, if 36 was called out, you might choose the two numbers 6 and 6 or 9 and 4.
- Correct numbers inside the hoop score five points each.
- Play this a number of times until everyone has had a go.
- The winners are the group with the most points after a given time.

NOW TRY THIS

Your teacher could call out a division sum for you to solve. You run to place the quotient inside the hoop, including a remainder.

MULTIPLE MOVE IT

OBJECTIVE: to improve ability to multiply any number
LEARNING LINK: visual, auditory, tactile
ORGANISATION: whole class
RESOURCES: none required

WHAT TO DO

- Walk quickly around the hall without bumping into anyone. Listen out for a times table number.
- If you hear a number in the five-times table, stand on one leg. If you hear a number in the six-times table, sit crossed-legged. If you hear a number in the seven-times table, lay down with arms outstretched. If you hear a number in the eight-times table, stand with your back to the wall.
- Remember: your teacher might call out numbers that are part of more than one times table. For example, 35 would mean standing on one leg and then laying down with arms outstretched and so on.

NOW TRY THIS

Alter the movements to be made and change the times tables.

IN A SPIN

OBJECTIVE: to improve ability to multiply any number
LEARNING LINK: visual, auditory, tactile
ORGANISATION: pairs
RESOURCES: coloured bibs

WHAT TO DO

- Get into pairs and gather in the hall.
- Get into two groups – the fives and the sixes. The fives could wear bibs of one colour and the sixes could wear a different colour.
- Move around the hall and listen out for a number.
- If your teacher calls out a multiple of 5, then the fives have to run around a number six and then crawl under their legs. For example, if the number 15 was called out, a five player runs round a six player three times (because $3 \times 5 = 15$), and then crawls under their legs.
- If a multiple of 6 is called out, for example 24, then all number sixes run around a number five four times (because $4 \times 6 = 24$), and then crawl under their legs.
- Repeat a number of times and look out for numbers like 30 and 60. What happens then?

NOW TRY THIS

Vary the movements that have to be performed. For example, instead of going round a partner and crawling under their legs, children could clap hands together.

PASS THE PARCEL

OBJECTIVE: to improve ability to multiply any number
LEARNING LINK: visual, auditory, tactile
ORGANISATION: whole class
RESOURCES: a box; newspaper; a sheet of wrapping paper; two dice labelled 3, 4, 5, 6, 7, 8; a bar of chocolate (or some other gift), in about ten layers of paper as 'pass the parcel' with gift wrap as the last layer

WHAT TO DO

- Sit in a circle and listen to a short snippet of music.
- When the music stops, the child holding the parcel rolls both dice. The two numbers thrown are then multiplied together. If that child works out the correct product, they can remove a layer of newspaper and the game continues.
- Repeat until the last layer of wrapping has been removed.

- The winner keeps the present – or the present can be shared between everyone!

NOW TRY THIS

Instead of a gift in the middle you could have a problem for the whole class to solve!

SHIFT IT

OBJECTIVE: to improve ability to multiply any number
LEARNING LINK: visual, auditory, tactile
ORGANISATION: four groups
RESOURCES: different-coloured cards with a multiplication or division sum written on each (about ten for each group in separate colours – questions can be written as $6 \times 4 = ?$ or written out as word problems)

WHAT TO DO

- The cards are on your teacher's desk in separate piles.
- Divide into about four groups.
- At the word *Go*, one person from each group runs to your teacher's desk and takes a question card. They run with it back to the group.
- The groups discuss what the answer is and write it down on a separate piece of paper. They then run back with the question card and their answer for your teacher to check.
- If the answer is correct, another question card is taken. If the answer is incorrect, the runner returns to the group and tries again.
- The first group to complete all their questions wins.

NOW TRY THIS

This game can be played against the clock rather than against each other.

NUMBER REVELATION

OBJECTIVE: to improve ability to multiply any number
LEARNING LINK: visual, auditory, tactile
ORGANISATION: whole class
RESOURCES: 30 pieces of paper with a set of numbers written on them (numbers that can be made by multiplying 4, 5, 6, 7, 8, 9 by 4, 5, 6, 7, 8, 9); two dice labelled 4, 5, 6, 7, 8, 9

WHAT TO DO

- The pieces of paper are placed on the floor in a random order.
- Everyone sits in a circle.
- One child starts by throwing the dice.
- Whatever numbers they throw, they multiply together to make one of the numbers on the floor.
- This player then calls out the product and takes the paper showing the product.
- Points are scored according to the product made.
- The player with the biggest total wins.

NOW TRY THIS

Have a bonus score for particular numbers, such as square numbers.

CLAP TRAP STAMP

OBJECTIVE: to improve ability to multiply any number
LEARNING LINK: visual, auditory, tactile
ORGANISATION: whole class
RESOURCES: a dice labelled 4, 5, 6, 7, 8, 9

WHAT TO DO

- A child rolls the dice and whichever number is thrown, this becomes the 'Clap Trap number'.
- For example, if the number 8 is thrown, everyone in the class gets into a rhythm of two claps, chants 8, then everyone stamps their feet twice, chants 16, claps twice, chants 24, stamps twice, chants 32, and so on.
- When 8 × 12 has been reached, the dice is passed to someone else and the process is repeated.

NOW TRY THIS

This game could be played by introducing a third movement or increasing the number of claps and stamps.

MUSICAL FACTORS

OBJECTIVE: to improve ability to multiply any number
LEARNING LINK: visual, auditory
ORGANISATION: whole class
RESOURCES: some music

WHAT TO DO

- Walk around the room as music is being played.
- When the music stops, your teacher will call out a number, for example 8.
- Work out how many factors the number called out has (in this case it is 4) and get into a group that matches that number.
- This game is useful for learning prime numbers.
- The game can be repeated as many times as you like.

NOW TRY THIS

You could play this game with division sums. For example, your teacher calls out 24 ÷ 6 and you have to group together according to the quotient.

SPLOSH

OBJECTIVE: to improve ability to multiply any number
LEARNING LINK: visual, auditory, tactile
ORGANISATION: maths buddies
RESOURCES: none required

WHAT TO DO

- Face a partner and clench one fist, which is called a 'splosh'.
- One player starts off by placing their 'splosh' on the table saying, 'four sploshes' (or whatever times table you are practising).
- The next player puts their splosh on top and says the next multiple, for example 'eight sploshes'.

- Play continues until you reach the 10th, 11th or 12th multiple.
- Any mistakes made in making sploshes means starting again.

NOW TRY THIS

Instead of sploshes, you can invent names of your own. The multiples can be said backwards when the 12th multiple has been reached.

MUSICAL NUMBERS

OBJECTIVE: to improve ability to multiply any number
LEARNING LINK: visual, auditory, tactile
ORGANISATION: whole class
RESOURCES: sticky labels or numbered bibs numbered with numbers from 2–9; some music

WHAT TO DO

● Each child has a sticky label or numbered bib to wear.
● Gather in the hall. Walk around and listen to the music.
● When the music stops, the boys freeze. Girls listen out for a number that your teacher calls out.
● For example if you hear 24, the girls have to work out which two numbers multiply together to make 24. If they are one of those numbers, then they have to find a boy with a corresponding number to make a product of 24.
● Repeat this game a number of times with boys and girls taking it in turns to freeze.

NOW TRY THIS

You could award points to players who team up with each other successfully.

A ROUND OF NUMBERS

OBJECTIVE: to improve ability to multiply any number
LEARNING LINK: visual, auditory, tactile
ORGANISATION: whole class
RESOURCES: some music

WHAT TO DO

● Form two concentric circles with one half of the class facing outwards and the other half facing inwards.
● Listen to the music and the circles move around: the outside circle move clockwise and the inner circle move anticlockwise.
● When the music stops, everyone must exchange products with the person immediately opposite them according to what your teacher shouts out.

● For example, if *Sevens* is called out, players play verbal tennis exchanging products by saying 7, 14, 21, 28, and so on.
● After one minute, the music starts again and players move around in the circles until the music stops.

NOW TRY THIS

This game can be played for any times table. You can limit the number of people in each circle and play for longer than a minute.

BACK AND FORTH

OBJECTIVE: to improve ability to multiply any number
LEARNING LINK: visual, auditory, tactile
ORGANISATION: groups of five or six
RESOURCES: five hoops; 0–9 number cards; mini-whiteboard and dry marker

WHAT TO DO

● Organise yourselves into groups of five or six.
● Five hoops are placed at one end of the hall. Sit in your groups at the other end of the hall facing the hoops.
● Inside the hoops there are a set of 0–9 number cards
● Look at the product on your teacher's mini-whiteboard.
● One player from each group runs to the hoop to find a number that will make part of the multiplication sum needed to make this product. This player runs back to the group and shows everyone the number.
● The next person in the group runs to the hoop to find the other number that will join with the number already chosen to make the product. For example, suppose the number written on the whiteboard was 24, one player might run up and choose 6. This player runs back and tags someone in the team who runs to find the number 4 because 6 × 4 makes 24.
● This player runs back and the team stands in a line with the front player showing the two numbers chosen.
● The first team to make the product scores three points.
● Return the numbers to the hoops and play the game again.

NOW TRY THIS

To simplify this game make the target number a division sum. Children run to the hoop to find the quotient.

Name _____ Date _____

Multiplication grid

1	2	3	4	5	6	7	8	9	10
2	4	6	8	10	12	14	16	18	20
3	6	9	12	15	18	21	24	27	30
4	8	12	16	20	24	28	32	36	40
5	10	15	20	25	30	35	40	45	50
6	12	18	24	30	36	42	48	54	60
7	14	21	28	35	42	49	56	63	70
8	16	24	32	40	48	56	64	72	80
9	18	27	36	45	54	63	72	81	90
10	20	30	40	50	60	70	80	90	100

SCHOLASTIC
www.scholastic.co.uk

Name _____ Date _____

Hundred square

1	2	3	4	5	6	7	8	9	10
11	12	13	14	15	16	17	18	19	20
21	22	23	24	25	26	27	28	29	30
31	32	33	34	35	36	37	38	39	40
41	42	43	44	45	46	47	48	49	50
51	52	53	54	55	56	57	58	59	60
61	62	63	64	65	66	67	68	69	70
71	72	73	74	75	76	77	78	79	80
81	82	83	84	85	86	87	88	89	90
91	92	93	94	95	96	97	98	99	100

Name _____ Date _____

Factor sheet – all of the numbers 1–100

1: 1
2: 1, 2
3: 1, 3
4: 1, 2, 4
5: 1, 5
6: 1, 2, 3, 6
7: 1, 7
8: 1, 2, 4, 8
9: 1, 3, 9
10: 1, 2, 5, 10
11: 1, 11
12: 1, 2, 3, 4, 6, 12
13: 1, 13
14: 1, 2, 7, 14
15: 1, 3, 5, 15
16: 1, 2, 4, 8, 16
17: 1, 17
18: 1, 2, 3, 6, 9, 18
19: 1, 19
20: 1, 2, 4, 5, 10, 20
21: 1, 3, 7, 21
22: 1, 2, 11, 22
23: 1, 23
24: 1, 2, 3, 4, 6, 8, 12, 24
25: 1, 5, 25
26: 1, 2, 13, 26
27: 1, 3, 9, 27
28: 1, 2, 4, 7, 14, 28
29: 1, 29
30: 1, 2, 3, 5, 6, 10, 15, 30
31: 1, 31
32: 1, 2, 4, 8, 16, 32
33: 1, 3, 11, 33
34: 1, 2, 17, 34
35: 1, 5, 7, 35
36: 1, 2, 3, 4, 6, 9, 12, 18, 36

37: 1, 37
38: 1, 2, 19, 38
39: 1, 3, 13, 39
40: 1, 2, 4, 5, 8, 10, 20, 40
41: 1, 41
42: 1, 2, 3, 6, 7, 14, 21, 42
43: 1, 43
44: 1, 2, 4, 11, 22, 44
45: 1, 3, 5, 9, 15, 45
46: 1, 2, 23, 46
47: 1, 47
48: 1, 2, 3, 4, 6, 8, 12, 16, 24, 48
49: 1, 7, 49
50: 1, 2, 5, 10, 25, 50
51: 1, 3, 17, 51
52: 1, 2, 4, 13, 26, 52
53: 1, 53
54: 1, 2, 3, 6, 9, 18, 27, 54
55: 1, 5, 11, 55
56: 1, 2, 4, 7, 8, 14, 28, 56
57: 1, 3, 19, 57
58: 1, 2, 29, 58
59: 1, 59
60: 1, 2, 3, 4, 5, 6, 10, 12, 15, 20, 30, 60
61: 1, 61
62: 1, 2, 31, 62
63: 1, 3, 7, 9, 21, 63
64: 1, 2, 4, 8, 16, 32, 64
65: 1, 5, 13, 65
66: 1, 2, 3, 6, 11, 22, 33, 66
67: 1, 67
68: 1, 2, 4, 17, 34, 68
69: 1, 3, 23, 69

70: 1, 2, 5, 7, 10, 14, 35, 70
71: 1, 71
72: 1, 2, 3, 4, 6, 8, 9, 12, 18, 24, 36, 72
73: 1, 73
74: 1, 2, 37, 74
75: 1, 3, 5, 15, 25, 75
76: 1, 2, 4, 19, 38, 76
77: 1, 7, 11, 77
78: 1, 2, 3, 6, 13, 26, 39, 78
79: 1, 79
80: 1, 2, 4, 5, 8, 10, 16, 20, 40, 80
81: 1, 3, 9, 27, 81
82: 1, 2, 41, 82
83: 1, 83
84: 1, 2, 3, 4, 6, 7, 12, 14, 21, 28, 42, 84
85: 1, 5, 17, 85
86: 1, 2, 43, 86
87: 1, 3, 29, 87
88: 1, 2, 4, 8, 11, 22, 44, 88
89: 1, 89
90: 1, 2, 3, 5, 6, 9, 10, 15, 18, 30, 45, 90
91: 1, 7, 13, 91
92: 1, 2, 4, 23, 46, 92
93: 1, 3, 31, 93
94: 1, 2, 47, 94
95: 1, 5, 19, 95
96: 1, 2, 3, 4, 6, 8, 12, 16, 24, 32, 48, 96
97: 1, 97
98: 1, 2, 7, 14, 49, 98
99: 1, 3, 9, 11, 33, 99
100: 1, 2, 4, 5, 10, 20, 25, 50, 100

Factor factoid

All numbers have an even number of factors unless they are square numbers. All square numbers have an odd number of factors.

Square, triangular, pentagonal and hexagonal numbers

Square numbers:

$1^2 = 1$	$11^2 = 121$	$21^2 = 441$	$31^2 = 961$	$41^2 = 1681$
$2^2 = 4$	$12^2 = 144$	$22^2 = 484$	$32^2 = 1024$	$42^2 = 1764$
$3^2 = 9$	$13^2 = 169$	$23^2 = 529$	$33^2 = 1089$	$43^2 = 1849$
$4^2 = 16$	$14^2 = 196$	$24^2 = 576$	$34^2 = 1156$	$44^2 = 1936$
$5^2 = 25$	$15^2 = 225$	$25^2 = 625$	$35^2 = 1225$	$45^2 = 2025$
$6^2 = 36$	$16^2 = 256$	$26^2 = 676$	$36^2 = 1296$	$46^2 = 2116$
$7^2 = 49$	$17^2 = 289$	$27^2 = 729$	$37^2 = 1369$	$47^2 = 2209$
$8^2 = 64$	$18^2 = 324$	$28^2 = 784$	$38^2 = 1444$	$48^2 = 2304$
$9^2 = 81$	$19^2 = 361$	$29^2 = 841$	$39^2 = 1521$	$49^2 = 2401$
$10^2 = 100$	$20^2 = 400$	$30^2 = 900$	$40^2 = 1600$	$50^2 = 2500$

Triangular numbers:

1	3	6	10	15	21	28	36	45	55
66	78	91	105	120	136	153	171	190	210
231	253	276	300	325	351	378	406	435	465
496	528	561	595	630	666	703	741	780	820
861	903	946	990	1035	1081	1128	1176	1225	1275
1326	1378	1431	1485	1540	1596	1653	1711	1770	1830
1891	1953	2016	2080	2145	2211	2278	2346	2415	2485
2556	2628	2701	2775	2850	2926	3003	3081	3160	3240
3321	3403	3486	3570	3655	3741	3828	3916	4005	4095
4186	4278	4371	4465	4560	4656	4753	4851	4950	5050

The sequence of the triangular numbers comes from the natural numbers (and zero), if you always add the next number:

$$1$$
$$1 + 2 = 3$$
$$(1 + 2) + 3 = 6$$
$$(1 + 2 + 3) + 4 = 10$$
$$(1 + 2 + 3 + 4) + 5 = 15$$

Pentagonal numbers:

1, 5, 12, 22, 35, 51, 70, 92, 117, 145, 176, 210, 247, 287, 330, 376, 425, 477, 532, 590, 651, 715, 782, 852, 925, 1001

(Every pentagonal number is one third of a triangular number.)

Hexagonal numbers:

1, 6, 15, 28, 45, 66, 91, 120, 153, 190, 231, 276, 325, 378, 435, 496, 561, 630, 703, 780, 861, 946

(Every hexagonal number is a triangular number, but not every triangular number is a hexagonal number.)

Octagonal numbers:

1, 8, 21, 40, 65, 96, 133, 176, 225, 280, 341, 408, 481, 560, 645, 736, 833, 936

Name _____ Date _____

Multiplication and division facts up to 10

0 x 1 = 0	0 x 3 = 0	0 x 5 = 0	0 x 7 = 0	0 x 9 = 0
1 x 1 = 1	1 x 3 = 3	1 x 5 = 5	1 x 7 = 7	1 x 9 = 9
2 x 1 = 2	2 x 3 = 6	2 x 5 = 10	2 x 7 = 14	2 x 9 = 18
3 x 1 = 3	3 x 3 = 9	3 x 5 = 15	3 x 7 = 21	3 x 9 = 27
4 x 1 = 4	4 x 3 = 12	4 x 5 = 20	4 x 7 = 28	4 x 9 = 36
5 x 1 = 5	5 x 3 = 15	5 x 5 = 25	5 x 7 = 35	5 x 9 = 45
6 x 1 = 6	6 x 3 = 18	6 x 5 = 30	6 x 7 = 42	6 x 9 = 54
7 x 1 = 7	7 x 3 = 21	7 x 5 = 35	7 x 7 = 49	7 x 9 = 63
8 x 1 = 8	8 x 3 = 24	8 x 5 = 40	8 x 7 = 56	8 x 9 = 72
9 x 1 = 9	9 x 3 = 27	9 x 5 = 45	9 x 7 = 63	9 x 9 = 81
10 x 1 = 10	10 x 3 = 30	10 x 5 = 50	10 x 7 = 70	10 x 9 = 90

0 ÷ 1 = 0	0 ÷ 3 = 0	0 ÷ 5 = 0	0 ÷ 7 = 0	0 ÷ 9 = 0
1 ÷ 1 = 1	3 ÷ 3 = 1	5 ÷ 5 = 1	7 ÷ 7 = 1	9 ÷ 9 = 1
2 ÷ 1 = 2	6 ÷ 3 = 2	10 ÷ 5 = 2	14 ÷ 7 = 2	18 ÷ 9 = 2
3 ÷ 1 = 3	9 ÷ 3 = 3	15 ÷ 5 = 3	21 ÷ 7 = 3	27 ÷ 9 = 3
4 ÷ 1 = 4	12 ÷ 3 = 4	20 ÷ 5 = 4	28 ÷ 7 = 4	36 ÷ 9 = 4
5 ÷ 1 = 5	15 ÷ 3 = 5	25 ÷ 5 = 5	35 ÷ 7 = 5	45 ÷ 9 = 5
6 ÷ 1 = 6	18 ÷ 3 = 6	30 ÷ 5 = 6	42 ÷ 7 = 6	54 ÷ 9 = 6
7 ÷ 1 = 7	21 ÷ 3 = 7	35 ÷ 5 = 7	49 ÷ 7 = 7	63 ÷ 9 = 7
8 ÷ 1 = 8	24 ÷ 3 = 8	40 ÷ 5 = 8	56 ÷ 7 = 8	72 ÷ 9 = 8
9 ÷ 1 = 9	27 ÷ 3 = 9	45 ÷ 5 = 9	63 ÷ 7 = 9	81 ÷ 9 = 9
10 ÷ 1 = 10	30 ÷ 3 = 10	50 ÷5 = 10	70 ÷ 7 = 10	90 ÷ 9 = 10

0 x 2 = 0	0 x 4 = 0	0 x 6 = 0	0 x 8 = 0	0 x 10 = 0
1 x 2 = 2	1 x 4 = 4	1 x 6 = 6	1 x 8 = 8	1 x 10 = 10
2 x 2 = 4	2 x 4 = 8	2 x 6 = 12	2 x 8 = 16	2 x 10 = 20
3 x 2 = 6	3 x 4 = 12	3 x 6 = 18	3 x 8 = 24	3 x 10 = 30
4 x 2 = 8	4 x 4 = 16	4 x 6 = 24	4 x 8 = 32	4 x 10 = 40
5 x 2 = 10	5 x 4 = 20	5 x 6 = 30	5 x 8 = 40	5 x 10 = 50
6 x 2 = 12	6 x 4 = 24	6 x 6 = 36	6 x 8 = 48	6 x 10 = 60
7 x 2 = 14	7 x 4 = 28	7 x 6 = 42	7 x 8 = 56	7 x 10 = 70
8 x 2 = 16	8 x 4 = 32	8 x 6 = 48	8 x 8 = 64	8 x 10 = 80
9 x 2 = 18	9 x 4 = 36	9 x 6 = 54	9 x 8 = 72	9 x 10 = 90
10 x 2 = 20	10 x 4 = 40	10 x 6 = 60	10 x 8 = 80	10 x 10 = 100

0 ÷ 2 = 0	0 ÷ 4 = 0	0 ÷ 6 = 0	0 ÷ 8 = 0	0 ÷ 10 = 0
2 ÷ 2 = 1	4 ÷ 4 = 1	6 ÷ 6 = 1	8 ÷ 8 = 1	10 ÷ 10 = 1
4 ÷ 2 = 2	8 ÷ 4 = 2	12 ÷ 6 = 2	16 ÷ 8 = 2	20 ÷ 10 = 2
6 ÷ 2 = 3	12 ÷ 4 = 3	18 ÷ 6 = 3	24 ÷ 8 = 3	30 ÷ 10 = 3
8 ÷ 2 = 4	16 ÷ 4 = 4	24 ÷ 6 = 4	32 ÷ 8 = 4	40 ÷ 10 = 4
10 ÷ 2 = 5	20 ÷ 4 = 5	30 ÷ 6 = 5	40 ÷ 8 = 5	50 ÷ 10 = 5
12 ÷ 2 = 6	24 ÷ 4 = 6	36 ÷ 6 = 6	48 ÷ 8 = 6	60 ÷ 10 = 6
14 ÷ 2 = 7	28 ÷ 4 = 7	42 ÷ 6 = 7	56 ÷ 8 = 7	70 ÷ 10 = 7
16 ÷ 2 = 8	32 ÷ 4 = 8	48 ÷ 6 = 8	64 ÷ 8 = 8	80 ÷ 10 = 8
18 ÷ 2 = 9	36 ÷ 4 = 9	54 ÷ 6 = 9	72 ÷ 8 = 9	90 ÷ 10 = 9
20 ÷ 2 = 10	40 ÷ 4 = 10	60 ÷ 6 = 10	80 ÷ 8 = 10	100 ÷ 10 = 10

■SCHOLASTIC
www.scholastic.co.uk

DAILY TIMES TABLES TEASERS FOR AGES 7–11

Name _____ Date _____

Napier's bones

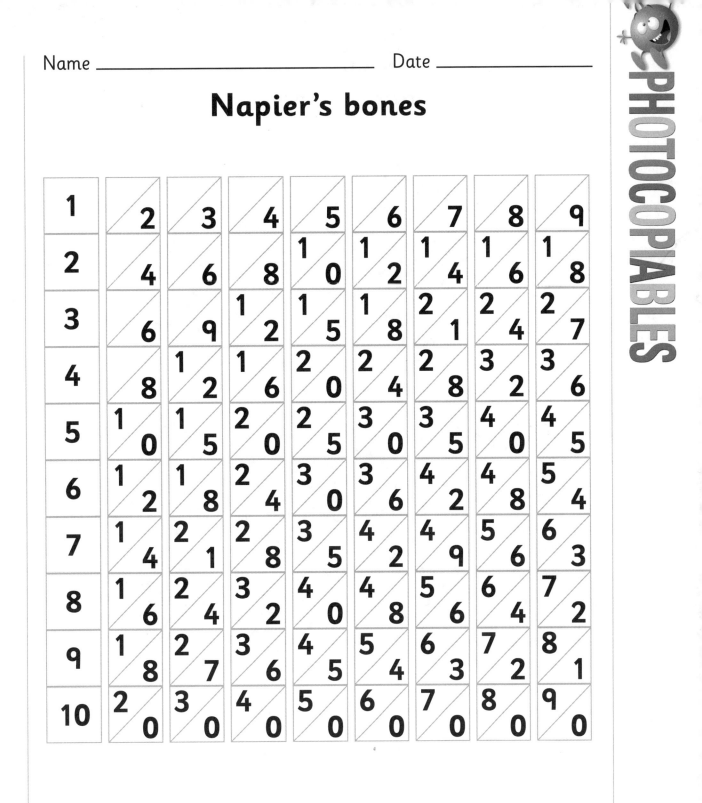

1	2	3	4	5	6	7	8	9
2	4	6	8	10	12	14	16	18
3	6	9	12	15	18	21	24	27
4	8	12	16	20	24	28	32	36
5	10	15	20	25	30	35	40	45
6	12	18	24	30	36	42	48	54
7	14	21	28	35	42	49	56	63
8	16	24	32	40	48	56	64	72
9	18	27	36	45	54	63	72	81
10	20	30	40	50	60	70	80	90

SCHOLASTIC
www.scholastic.co.uk

Also available in this series:

ISBN 978-0439-94543-1

ISBN 978-0439-94544-8

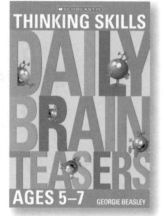

ISBN 978-0439-96542-2

ISBN 978-0439-96543-9

ISBN 978-0439-96544-6

To find out more, call: 0845 603 9091
or visit our website www.scholastic.co.uk